'No one can forget the images of 1 incredulity, pain and helplessness at tl This book is a fitting testament to resilient community caught up in an catastrophe. Gaby weaves her family's own stoi y ... that describes the events from many perspectives and points to the way in which ordinary people responded to promptings to "do something" with remarkable and life-changing effects. The pain and sorrow are palpable but Gaby also infuses the pages with warmth, humour, realism and, above all, hope.'

Caroline Welby

'This book does not gloss over the tragedy, the bitterness and the hard political questions that surround the devastating fire at Grenfell Tower. But by telling the stories of individuals, allowing them their voice, Gaby Doherty shows us that there is always hope. Hope challenges the past and the present, demanding change; hope energizes, enables and refuses to be silent. This is a powerful, challenging and hopeful book, but only if we are prepared to take our part, not to stand by as onlookers.'

Dr Jane Williams, Assistant Dean, St Mellitus College

'Ordinary people lost their lives and homes in the horrendous Grenfell Tower disaster. Ordinary people have also picked up the task of support and survival, working for a more hopeful future for others caught up in the system of unfairness and neglect. Gaby Doherty sees herself as an ordinary person, but, like many of those she writes about, has a vision for justice rooted in powerful faith and hope. The multiple personal narratives in this compassionate book are woven skilfully together to produce a challenging reminder of the significance of people's lives and communities, and to make us resolved to work for a future which is more just and loving.'

Dr Elaine Storkey, author of Scars Across Humanity: Understanding and overcoming violence against women

'Gaby Doherty writes movingly from first-hand experience of the Grenfell Tower fire and its aftermath. Without minimizing the horror of what happened, she tells stories of hope in the midst of tragedy.'

The Revd Nicky Gumbel, vicar, Holy Trinity Brompton

'If you want to hear the stories from Grenfell Tower, read this book and read it with your church. Psalm 95 talks about hearing the Lord's voice and not hardening your heart. Gaby helps us to hear echoes of that voice from that night and the days that followed. She asks about our response. From that terrible night have emerged stories of faith, hope and love.'

The Rt Revd Keith Sinclair, Bishop of Birkenhead

'From her bedroom window, Gaby Doherty watched, horrified, as Grenfell Tower burned. Although stunned, she sprang into action in her community, sharing with others the grief, outrage and pain caused by the fire. *Grenfell Hope* contains not only her heartfelt account but gives voice to those often overlooked or misrepresented in the media. She shares stories of hope and transformation as ordinary people unite in extraordinary ways. And she reveals how neighbours bear each other's burdens in Christ and how God reveals his presence in times of great pain. Don't miss this previously untold story.'

Amy Boucher Pye, author of Finding Myself in Britain: Our search for faith, home and true identity

'How do we offer hope when disaster comes to our door? In this timely book, Doherty offers a rare perspective: the eyewitness accounts of the political leaders and religious communities, and how they helped on the ground. This is not a book full of "grief tourism", but an exploration of the good – and bad – ordinary people can do. The book identifies unexpected heroes who love justice, look at suffering square on and don't offer glib answers, but look for practical good and supernatural hope. As someone active in the hub of support after the Grenfell fire, Doherty not only writes hope, she lives it. She is the perfect person to present this treasury of shards of hope within the wreckage, and she does so with grace and humility. Read it for lament, not hand-wringing; intelligent critique, not outrage; a vision of justice, not despair – and above all, read it to be inspired by ordinary people, and reflect on what it means to be a hope-bearer in this world.'

Tanya Marlow, campaigner for health equality and author of Those Who Wait: Finding God in disappointment, doubt and delay

'Gaby and I both believe in the efficacy of hope. We both believe that the lives that were lost will not have been in vain.'

Counsellor Judith Blakeman, Royal Borough of Kensington and Chelsea

Gaby Doherty is a wife to Sean and mum to four children. She is passionate about faith, friends and justice, and speaking and writing about them. She hopes to leave the world a better place because she has lived. This is her first book.

GRENFELL
HOPE

Stories from the community

Gaby Doherty

First published in Great Britain in 2018

Society for Promoting Christian Knowledge
36 Causton Street
London SW1P 4ST
www.spck.org.uk

British Library Cataloguing-in-Publication Data
A catalogue record for this book is available from the British Library

ISBN 978–0–281–07962–9
eBook ISBN 978–0–281–07963–6

Typeset by Geethik, India
First printed in Great Britain by Jellyfish Print Solutions
Subsequently digitally reprinted in Great Britain

eBook by Geethik, India

Produced on paper from sustainable forests

*This book is dedicated with love
to the colourful community of North Kensington*

Contents

Preface

In writing a book called *Grenfell Hope* there have been a number of issues.

First, hope is hard to find in times like this. We need hope, though, to retain our sanity and to encourage healing and forgiveness. Many people have told me that there is no hope; they are right that the fire was hopeless and nothing good can be found to say about death and suffering. However, I choose to believe that there can be hope in the wake of horror and tragedy.

Many beautiful people lost their lives. Behind each one of those is a grieving family, devastated friends and a bewildered community. Nothing that I write could ever make the events of that evening seem anything but devastating. But for myself, my family, my friends, I wanted to try to find hope and share it. Please don't for one moment think I have not cried tears of sadness over the stories of my friends and neighbours who died. I have obsessed over terrible web stories that told me about their last moments, their last conversations, and tried to second-guess their thoughts and feelings. I have woken up at 5 a.m. and planned my own fire escape routes and all the while thanked God for my own children and their safety.

There has been a personal cost in looking for hope. Some stories may seem small and insignificant when the reality is that at the time of writing few of the survivors have new homes yet. Many are still in hotels and temporary accommodation. The public inquiry and police enquiries are still under way. Yet one tragic day meant that humanity planted so many tiny seeds which grew into something precious. Isaiah 61 tells of beauty coming from ashes and the rebuilding of ancient ruins. This book is my attempt at discerning beauty among the ashes, and my prayer is that, whatever ashes you are facing, you too may find beauty from them in time.

My purpose is to tell the story from my perspective and share some of the stories of my friends. Hopefully these will encourage and inspire you to seek transformation in your own community, without the goad of a hideous tragedy. These stories are just a tiny pixel, just one perspective. The whole picture is much bigger and there are even more amazing stories to tell. Perhaps one day someone will capture the rest of it. I simply offer the Grenfell Hope that I have seen and experienced.

Acknowledgements

This whole project has been a 'God idea' from the start, and all thanks and praise go to him.

Thanks to Amy Boucher-Pye who suggested the whole project and believed in me enough to tout the idea to the publisher.

I would like to thank Sean, my husband, for his never-ending encouragement and love – and for letting me go away for two nights to finish off the book!

I would also like to thank my family, especially my Mumma and mother-in-law who have looked after the children endlessly and have helped us live this crazy life in London. Thanks go to Zaila Dunbar and Tanya Marlow who read my toughest chapter and gave helpful pointers (which involved completely restructuring the whole chapter!), and to Lizzie Jakeman who gave me free counselling and put me in touch with Ruth Divall, whose depth of knowledge and understanding about Christian hope was a deep well I drew from.

Finally, I am grateful to all those who gave me their time so generously for interview, despite this being a very tough, personal subject.

Note to the reader

All royalties from this book will go to support the continuing work of St Clement and St James Church of England School, Penzance Place, Kensington. For more information about the school, go to <www.scsj.rbkc.sch.uk>.

1

Introduction

At 9 p.m. on Friday, 9 June 2017, my husband tore over to the open window of our bedroom and shouted, in as close to a football-hooligan roar as I have heard him make, 'Kensington, you beauty!' He doesn't usually partake in uncouth gestures. He's a Reverend Doctor, a tutor in ethics at an Anglican theological college, and a local church minister.

But he wasn't the only one. Others all over the borough were rejoicing – and not those who normally get a chance to celebrate the result of a general election.

This was the moment when, after three recounts, Emma Dent Coad was declared to be the new Labour Member of Parliament in this fairly young constituency of Kensington and Chelsea. Twenty years of Conservative leadership had taken its toll on the people of the area and we were ready to party. Families celebrated outside Kensington Town Hall, where we saw drummers and dancing.

We were ready for change. We might have lost the war but our own area of battle was won, and Lady (Victoria) Borwick, the previous MP and former Deputy Mayor of London, had to step aside gracefully.

The disquiet which led to this result had been building for some time. From my vantage point at the school gate, I sensed the local mums becoming restless. I heard much talk in playgrounds of how the state of this borough could not continue. We were dissatisfied with the grants our school received, with the lack of financing, let alone the investment that had not gone into the National Health Service (NHS), and with the increasing gap between those in my neighbourhood and the wealthy next door, who seemed to view the rest of us as their workforce with the arrogance that wealth allows.

The Monday after the results, I hugged a few other mums in the playground, buoyant in our success. Each of us felt our vote had counted. Each of us was jubilant that we had encouraged others to bother with voting, and how that had made a difference. We were relieved that we were able to face our many local friends who couldn't vote because of their immigration status or lack of citizenship. We had won the battle they wished they could fight.

The excitement lasted into the next week as we gossiped about what change this might make for us as a borough and how it was time the ruling Conservatives had a shake-up.

Days later, in the early hours of 14 June, I woke abruptly from the noise of my husband moving around again. As it was 1.30 a.m., I berated him for going to bed so late. He said, 'I'm not going to bed; I'm getting up. Grenfell is on fire. I'm going to see what I can do to help.'

I rushed to the window and could hear the sirens and smoke alarms, and see the flames racing up the side of the building.

Sean asked me to send our friends' phone number to him but I said I'd ring myself. It felt like a scene from a film, but much scarier because we didn't know whether there would be a happy ending. We had no assurance that the daring firefighters would put out the blaze. All we could see was a massive building being engulfed by fire with flames that were perhaps a hundred feet high and devouring everything quickly.

As Sean left, wearing his clergy dog collar, I tried to ring my friend. It was 1.50 a.m. and her phone went straight to answerphone. I left a desperate text message, praying that she and her family, her husband and her three-year-old daughter were all somewhere safe. I also had another friend for whom I had no contact details, nor was I sure where she lived, but I knew it was very close to the Tower. Both families filled my head and my heart.

The flames were horrific and I couldn't help but watch as the hungry fire devoured the defenceless building. Helicopters hung overhead, and the sirens screamed and didn't stop for many hours. I shut all the windows in the house, anxious that the smoky air would poison my children – the same way it was poisoning other people's babies 200 metres away.

I tried to ring my friend again. I sent her another message, then sat on my bed and prayed. I watched the night turn to day and the Tower turn from light bright flames to dark charred space with the flames still burning.

As the dawn broke, my friends woke up all around the area and started sending messages. We all live dotted around the

Tower. Some of us could see it; some were hearing the helicopters and saw the flames on the television, confused and horrified that such a familiar landmark was actually burning.

From my place of safety I had no choice but to watch what was happening just over the road.

I sat on my bed and prayed and messaged and watched and listened to the fire burn. I was blessed because 200 metres was far enough away that I didn't hear or see much of the detail. Some of my friends lived closer, and saw things no one should ever see. Adults as well as children were paralysed with fear as the fire ripped through. None of us could take our eyes off the red poison engulfing the building that housed so many.

So many questions still weren't answered. Who was safe? Who was perishing? How many souls were lost, we wondered, as we watched helplessly and prayed.

Terrible things were happening too, such as people jumping out in a last-ditch attempt to survive. To my knowledge none of them did.

I wandered outside at one point and found the neighbours of my block standing around variously attired. I was in my pyjamas. We all expressed our incredulity and spoke of those we knew who lived in Grenfell Tower. My upstairs neighbour was the first to receive good news of her friend and three kids, who were all safe and sound at Latymer Community Church. They were dazed and confused, but unhurt and out of harm's way. Another of my neighbours had a friend on the Tower's twelfth floor. She was in tears of fear. What was happening to her friend? I later discovered her friend was fine.

In my heart I knew my own friend and her family were not fine. Every moment that I didn't receive a message over the next few days clarified this for me. No one had seen them. Not even her sister had heard from them. Then we heard the devastating news that all those in hospital had been identified. My friends were gone.

At 3.21 a.m. I emailed the manager and staff at my daughter's nursery, which my friend's child also attended, asking them to pray if they received the email.

As the dawn arrived, the fire was still fierce. At 5.45 a.m. my ten-year-old daughter awoke as normal and I called her through to my room. I broke the news as gently as I could. She looked up from where she sat on my bed and said, 'But Mummy, lots of people live in that building.' She burst into tears and I tried to comfort her. We were united in grief, even though we didn't fully know what we were grieving. We only knew we had already lost something very important.

In the days to follow, this unity in grief became a common theme for our community.

2

Waking up

The sun had risen, day had dawned, and it was as if someone had hit 'pause' on my life.

I sat and prayed, my eyes still drawn to the attention-seeking fire which had to be the centre of every conversation in every home, as it would be for weeks after.

My daughter Jemie, aged ten, wanted to do something to help, so I sent her with milk, cereal and a blanket over the road to Latymer Community Church. She felt better after she came back as she had done something positive. She told me she'd seen a whole window frame on fire go crashing to the ground.

My eight-year-old son, Joey, woke not long after. His first question was, 'Can you pinch me, Mummy, because I think I'm still asleep?' His second question was, 'Is it terrorists, Mummy?' I didn't know but I prayed that it wouldn't be! *Please God, let this evil not be a result of human planning. Please let it be an accident.* We didn't know what had caused the fire at this point, but the terror threat chilled me to the core.

Caleb, my five-year-old, was scared of the flames. He was petrified they would spread to us and burn us up. He carried on being scared for the next 24 hours as the unquenchable fires continued. He kept checking continually out of the window.

'Have the flames stopped yet, Mummy?'

'No, not yet, darling, but they will.'

The following night he would prove impossible to settle as he kept hopping out of bed to look out of the window to check on the status of the fire. The blaze did not die down until mid-afternoon on the second day after it began, a constant reminder of the night of horrors and our helplessness and pain. By 10 p.m. Caleb decided that when he was older he would like to be a fireman or a policeman so he could help people; we had all seen the fantastic way in which the emergency services were working.

My three-year-old, Esther, was more interested in the human element when she woke up. 'Is that Simona's house?' she asked, as just that weekend we'd been at a birthday party for a lovely Eritrean child in the tower block behind us.

'No, darling, I'm sorry to tell you that is Amaya's house and she may have been hurt in the fire.'

She seemed to take it all in her stride, but the next weeks would be full of continual questions and comments and statements about Amaya and the fire. Every time she saw it, the Tower would spark a new conversation, sometimes about how Amaya had died or who she had been with. Sometimes Esther created another reality in which Amaya got out and survived. She told me Amaya was in heaven. She told me she was angry with the firefighters for not saving Amaya. She told me that the police didn't know where to look for Amaya but we did because she's in heaven. She spoke of it being hard to get people back from the dead because she didn't know any fairies who could help her. She asked, 'When there is a new creation, will Amaya be there?' She drew pictures. She and Caleb even shared their grief, one day, by saying they were going to poo on the Tower, making it an object of ridicule, not the scary beast that had killed Esther's friend but something they could mock. They also spent time making a book of pictures of Amaya and her family. We made a photo album with pictures of lots of her friends, and a special photo of her and Amaya, and all these things helped, but she still continued to talk and ask and suppose.

At times Esther's blunt questioning had me in tears, but this didn't thwart her, fortunately, as she continued vociferously to explore grief and what it meant to her. She never stopped poking and prodding at this sensitive place. Her perseverance and love for her friend were obvious and admirable.

The news spread on social media, on networks of friends and through the press. People in the USA knew before most of the UK because many Americans were just going to bed as we were still waking up. CNN was on the scene. Many journalists and newspeople live in the area so they started filing reports as quickly as they could. Most had one question: how did the fire spread so fast?

Everything around us started closing in. Our world became smaller. Roads, paths, streets and even our postboxes were closed. Police swarmed in to help. The tube and buses were not running. We became a tiny microcosm unto ourselves which the whole world wanted to visit, some through their television screens, others in real life. It was starting to become like a parallel universe.

I walked the children to school slightly earlier than usual. I momentarily considered keeping them at home, but we had nothing better to do than watch the flames, which didn't seem to be a good idea. Our route was busier than normal because so many roads were closed. People coming to work in the industrial area nearby were staggering like drunkards as they surveyed the still-burning inferno.

As we neared the school the heat of the day was becoming apparent, with temperatures soaring to 33 degrees Celsius. Many people across the country would be commenting on what a beautiful day it was, but to us the heat only magnified our pain by making the hours more unbearable and the fire officers' jobs that bit harder.

Our church had held its usual prayer gathering and we were gratified to hear how prayer had made a difference because someone was pulled still alive from the building at 7.30 a.m., just as the church folk were praying for that very thing. What joy we felt! Having seen the heat of the inferno that was still roaring, it was a miracle anyone got out alive.

All the way to school I was thinking about a family whose children attended the same school as mine. They lived either in or near Grenfell. Did they live in the Tower? Would they even be at the school gates any more? As we arrived at the entrance, there was an eerie silence and people were crying and hugging. Several parents turned around and took their kids home as they couldn't be parted from them on such a day. The family I was concerned about finally arrived, their two children still in pyjamas. They had been evacuated in the night but were fine. I was so relieved to see them. Even now it reduces me to tears.

They, like many other families from school, lived in one of the 'finger blocks' beneath Grenfell Tower. One family who were evacuated had a child with chickenpox. The poor boy was covered in spots – as if the parents didn't already have enough on their plates with a sick child.

As it happened, none of the children from our school lived in the Tower, although most had seen the fire in some form and many had seen it close up, smelt the smoke, reached out to suffering friends, felt the flames and heard the horrors. In Caleb's class one child spent the entire day making a big tower block and sticking flames down the side. The children wanted to engage through art with what was happening, and when mine came home I spent time with them, allowing them to draw and talk about how they felt. This has continued regularly since that day. These are memories that will haunt many for the rest of their lives.

When I'd dropped the kids at school I arranged with my friends that we should be together. Relief efforts came from all over, and the amount of items donated was picking up at an incredible pace, but so were the numbers of volunteers from outside who were coming into our area. There was no shortage of helping hands, so I thought it would be better for all of us who lived locally to stick together and have time to talk. In the end everyone came back to my garden.

Being together was really key for those first few days. We didn't want to be apart or leave our kids very far from us. One friend swept up the ash in my garden, and we endured the smell of smoke and drank tea. Even the husband of one of my friends came to join us as we sat and puzzled out how, what, who and why. *Who is alive? Who is missing?* Everything was happening so fast and, with newspeople reporting everything that moved and interviewing everyone they thought might count, it was a crazy time. All we wanted to know was: were our friends safe and how could this have happened?

One of my friends had children in both the schools most attended by the families who lived in the Tower. She knew two children from her four-year-old's class who were unaccounted for. One of them was found eventually in hospital. The other tragically died.

As my friends and I spent time together we grew closer, sharing our fears and an experience of pain that we had never had before. We sat and talked, had moments of stunned silence and just kept repeating the same things. 'How did this happen?' Fairly early on, the news reported that a fridge had exploded in one of the flats and then the outside cladding of the Tower caught fire, acting like a chimney as the insulation behind it burned.

As we sat in the heat of the boiling morning sun, our youngest children played innocently in the paddling pool in the back garden while the fire burned visibly in front of our homes. We were comforted by being together, but badly rattled: our safety was gone. Our friends were missing and it seemed as if part of our community had been destroyed. We tried to get our heads around what was happening.

At the same time, the very opposite to community destruction was happening. Our community was throwing up green shoots through the hard concrete of London life. Things were happening all around us that we couldn't appreciate at this point but which became apparent a few days later. The area was rising up, and its people were finding their voices and discovering new ways of expressing themselves. A wave of love was hitting the neighbourhood, showing itself in a thousand different details. Out of this tragedy, love was growing and people were not afraid to show it.

Life began to pick up speed and things became increasingly weird. Old patterns of reserve started to break down. Every person I even barely recognized was someone I had to greet. As we passed each other in the street we offered a quick kind word or a comforting thought.

We shared stories of our loved ones missing since the fire. Neighbours wondered about whole families whom no one had seen. Often the same stories were shared, the same questions raised, but from a different perspective. I discovered connection after connection, making new friends through missing friends.

The first person who mentioned heaven to me was a young Muslim man I know from the estate. Our conversation is normally limited to 'You all right?', 'I'm well, thanks'. He was relieved that those who had died would be in heaven as it's a better place, and I agreed – this was not a time to discuss our theology!

The pain of the loss had not even hit us at that point. Those who visited grieved and cried for us, but mostly we locals walked around dazed, with sunken horror-filled looks on our faces. I didn't smile for days. Smiling just didn't come. I remember trying to crack a smile just to see if I still could, but it was forced and false. By 9 a.m. on the day of the fire almost every clergy person in the district was on hand to help, including the Bishop. Local celebrities were interviewed by the constantly present camera crews who kept us in the news for weeks after; they couldn't stay away. Then ordinary people began to flood in. Grief tourists, I called them. They wanted to see, feel, smell and process this tragedy. How could this have happened?

People couldn't arrive by public transport because initially it was all shut down, and the roads were closed. So they walked. The railings became festooned with flowers and tributes. Latymer Community Church became a central focus because it started up a memory wall, but there wasn't just one memory wall. The whole area became a memory walk, with tributes surrounding the Tower at every church, community area and centre. People came to pay respects; they came to experience the weird atmosphere. The streets were filled with people, all asking 'Why?' They came to help. They came to cry. They came to rant and share their conspiracy theories.

And there was that silent spot on Bramley Road, directly in line with my bedroom, which afforded an overwhelming view of the Tower. That spot was where everyone stood and looked. It was as if there was an unspoken rule to be silent there.

Then 'missing' posters began to appear. Relatives and friends made pictures of their loved ones and stuck them up everywhere. People were desperate to know what had happened to family and friends. Were they in hospital? Had they somehow escaped and failed to tell people? That was in fact the story of one family who had escaped the flames. They went off to a friend's house and didn't think to tell anyone they were safe. The matter was cleared up after a few days, but tragically this was not the story for most of the missing.

I was walking home with the children the following Friday and came face to face with a poster of my daughter's friend Amaya, with 'Missing' on it. Someone had attached a bunch of yellow roses to the tree. I started to cry. I couldn't stop myself. The children were visibly shaken as this is not my normal behaviour. I tried to explain it was from the shock of seeing her face so unexpectedly. The photo was from Amaya's third birthday party just a few months before. We had been honoured to be the only British people at the party – everyone else was

Eritrean. As we walked home, more posters appeared. Esther commented on every single one!

This became my daughter's pattern for the next few weeks, stopping at every poster of Amaya and commenting. Always asking questions, making statements: 'Amaya is my friend and she is missing. I don't want her to be dead.' 'I want to go to Amaya's flat so I can be dead and see Amaya again.'

Esther was probably one of those most comfortable with her grief. She just kept talking about it and sharing her pain. Many others, myself included, were struggling to know how we felt, but she just kept on processing, working through her sadness and pain. She still does. Sometimes on the way to school she'll say things like, 'Let's talk about Grenfell. We'll take it in turns.'

In all of this I am glad about the choices I made. I chose to spend time with my friends. I chose to care for those around me. I chose which meetings to go to and when to escape for the day or the week. When life deals you a bad hand, you will also have to make choices. God can fuel you, or you can forget him and blame him for the things that have gone wrong. I chose to submit and to be submerged in him. I prayed. I looked for purpose in everything. I chose to try to be joyful in the circumstances. I chose to try to help others where I could, but in all these things I tried to keep myself functioning, loving and healthy. If I collapsed, my family would too. Initially in the days following the fire I felt as if there was a tug to do more, work more, serve more. *There is so much to do – just get stuck in, Gaby!* And I did, to a certain extent, but all the character and biblical training I have had helped me to keep a healthy perspective. I reminded myself that although our neighbourhood was the focus of such great attention, eventually the furore would die down and we would be left as we were before, with limited resources and tired people serving God, so I knew for the sake of myself and my family that I had to keep some boundaries and save some energy.

This is the Christian gospel. We believe that we die with Christ, that we bear one another's burdens and weep with those who weep. This suffering is painful and there is no way around it. It is no surprise that our grief is exhausting and complicated. We were weeping and mourning, and people from surrounding communities were coming to bring us comfort.

The day of the fire wore on, with stories coming out of what was happening, horror stories for the most part, and then suddenly a moment of hope at about 2 p.m. Despite the fierce flames that were still roaring, a blind gentleman was rescued alive from the building. Amid so much pain, there was time to laugh and be filled with joy for this one saved soul. Donations of money and clothing and supplies had started racing in from everywhere. There was talk of people needing large cars to take boxes of provisions to the town hall. I offered my car for that evening.

Some of the simplest tasks became the hardest. The extreme heat of the day meant that walking back to school that afternoon was unpleasant, and when I got to my children they were all in a bad state. They were exhausted, scared and emotionally very fragile. We had discussed on the way to school how rumours would be rife from the other children and, sure enough, this proved to be the case. Some children were even pretending they had been in the fire and escaped.

My son Caleb was fixated by the flames and just wanted to keep watching until they were extinguished. We had a long, slow journey home as I unpicked the sadness from my children's day. It didn't help that we stopped to speak to and comfort every person we knew. It was just how things were. You don't pass bereaved people without telling them you are sorry for their loss, and offering love. The whole community was bereaved and at this early stage we were all shocked.

I tried to keep things normal, but how can you be normal when what you usually do on a Wednesday is go swimming at a leisure centre that is currently full of firefighters, underneath a still-burning building?

I went home instead and did some artwork with my little children, who asked to draw their feelings. All they wanted to do was draw a big tower on fire, interspersed with Caleb racing to the window to check if the burning had stopped.

When it came to bedtime our normal strict 'children to bed in their own bed' policy was shot to pieces. Esther was too scared to sleep alone. Caleb too woke in the middle of the night, and the next morning I opened my eyes to find one each side of me, cuddled up like kittens.

I had been awake since the early hours, and had only had a couple of hours' sleep, but before I called it a day I went off in my car to help move boxes. It was a wild goose chase that taught me a lot about where and how to place my energy in the coming weeks.

The compulsion to rush in is deeply rooted. During the fire my oldest daughter's first thought had been, 'What can I do to help?' She told me that by 6 a.m. there was already a huge amount of cereal and milk at Latymer Community Church. Obviously she wasn't the only one with that thought! This was just the start of the torrent of goodwill that was to follow.

If the kindness and provision had come simply from the local community, each of the survivors of this tragedy would have been well catered for. As it happened, the fire roused the kindness and generosity not only of our nation, but of the world.

As people awoke to the terrible images on their televisions, many were struck with a question: 'What can I do?' Often they came to a similar conclusion: that they should send or bring things to replace whatever was lost.

The churches began to receive donations of clothes, bedding and toiletries. The amounts started out small, arriving by the bagful, but there was something that touched people's hearts and affected them so profoundly about the burning building that they felt they had to do something.

Soon, more stuff was arriving than any number of people would need. The whole of Kensington was turning into a warehouse of old and new clothes, bedding, toys . . . and it just kept coming. I was at St James' Church, which was full to the rafters and yet still people kept bringing more. Volunteers tried politely to refuse it, but donors were sometimes insistent and refused to take their things back. They had driven a long way and they wanted to leave the items to help victims. No amount of pacifying them and explaining we were full would keep them from their goal.

I loaded my car full and set off to the recommended drop-off place, Kensington Town Hall. The traffic was awful and I had two cars of volunteers following me with boxes overflowing out of their cars too.

When we arrived at the town hall it was mayhem. It too was full and the workers were again turning away donations. Everything was changing so fast: it was hard for centres to keep up with the flood of items. As the second night wore on, the fire kept burning, still not fully extinguished, and the donations kept coming.

I manoeuvred around the traffic at the town hall and met a delightful man in a minibus who had come from east London with five vans full of provisions donated by a mosque there. Solidarity was growing quickly and people were getting stuck in. But where would all the donations go?

Meanwhile those who had lost their homes and families were still in complete shock. The donations acted as a good distraction, keeping people busy and away from those who were totally wrecked. There were high levels of uncertainty, because no one was able to say who was dead and who was missing or in hospital. The official figures claimed only six dead at this stage, but it was clear that this was only a drop in the ocean of sadness. My thoughts and prayers as I drove were for Amaya and her parents, Amal and Mo. I was praying that they were all unconscious in hospital, that they'd got out and left their phones at home. I knew this was a long shot as their next of kin had heard no word from them.

Despite hundreds of people offering accommodation to the survivors of the fire, very few of these proposals could be accepted. No matter how many kind people were offering spaces in their family homes, there was no way the authorities could agree to this, because it might mean placing very vulnerable people in unsafe situations. I found it strange that it was deemed safer to give people mattresses on a sports hall floor than in local residents' homes. Families and friends were stepping in and opening their doors, but the kindness of strangers could not be accepted.

The scale of the crisis was too big. It felt as if no one had taken charge at this point. Council workers were sent to help but told to remove their lanyards so they wouldn't bear the brunt of people's anger, which was rising towards the Tenant Management Organisation (TMO) and Kensington Borough Council. This then gave the impression that council workers were not on hand, when in fact many were; it's just that they didn't seem to be in charge or controlling the crisis. They didn't really know what to do. A friend who worked in the Council told me that no one had had experience of this kind of situation, or appropriate training.

The following days were amazing but crazy. Donations flowed in for the next week, and no amount of social media messages or signs outside churches, mosques and community centres could stop the lava flow of generosity. Sorting the donations became a full-time job for some, and I remember a local priest Father Alan and his congregation working ceaselessly to empty the church so that they could have mass as normal on the Sunday morning.

However, 'normal' was not a word that could be applied to the area – and still cannot. Everything had changed. We had changed with it and we were facing a dual challenge: the blessing of incredible generosity from thousands of people whose hearts had been moved to help and donate items; and the curse of what to do with it all, because it would be weeks and months before people would be moved to new homes. Many survivors lived in hotels for months after, as they waited for suitable accommodation in the already overcrowded borough that had just lost several hundred homes.

Two thousand years ago, the three wise men brought expensive gifts for the baby King Jesus. Inappropriate gifts for a baby, not ones that would help him teethe or keep him warm and dry, but symbolic gifts that represented his importance, his value, and his life and death. Gold showed his divinity and perhaps funded Mary and Joseph in their subsequent flight to Egypt. Frankincense suggests righteousness and perhaps signi- fied a burnt offering, foretelling Jesus' giving of himself as a sacrifice. Myrrh was used for embalming and perhaps pre- dicted the spices that were to be placed on Jesus' body after he died. At the time of the Grenfell fire, we could not always see the practical use of the tidal wave of donations that came in. But like the gifts of the wise men, these donations represented the love and care of the wider community and future provision for those who had lost everything.

This outpouring of generosity came at great cost too. The enormous number of individual offerings to Grenfell survivors showed that the public were thinking about the needs of those affected. These gifts represented the value the many donors attributed to other human beings. Some gave sacrificially, donat- ing things that they themselves needed. Howard Taylor, of the ClementJames Centre, told me later:

> There is a well-known local homeless man in the area who, due to his mental health concerns and alcohol dependency, is known to get quite loud and aggressive towards members of the public. He came to the ClementJames Centre about a week after the fire and we assumed he would be looking for donations that hadn't been given away that we could gift to him. In fact he wanted to donate his one and only coat, and despite us thanking him but saying he should keep it, he gave it to

go to a good home with one of the survivors. That really brought home to me how much the community had been affected by the fire.

Out of their treasures, people brought bedding, clothes and toiletries.

3

The cavalry wore dog collars

There are thousands of others who also have stories to tell about their experiences of 14 June 2017. Some of those are church leaders, and one is very special to me: Sean Doherty, my husband! Here is some of his story:

The night before the fire, I had gone to bed quite late. I hadn't been asleep long before I was woken by sirens. It's normal to hear sirens here at night and even sometimes a helicopter, especially around the time of the Notting Hill Carnival, but this was so many – more sirens than I have ever heard in my life before. I also became aware of a constant piercing beeping which I thought was a car alarm.

I got up and went to the window and as I opened the curtains I instantly had the shock of seeing Grenfell Tower engulfed in flames. It is right opposite our bedroom window and only about 250 metres away, so it absolutely dominated the view. There were huge flames shooting up what seemed like the whole left-hand side of the Tower so it was immediately obvious the fire was massive. As I watched, what was terrifying was how quickly it was spreading across the building. The beeping sound suddenly made sense as there must have been hundreds of smoke alarms going off in rooms throughout the Tower.

The most horrifying thing was that I could see so many people at their windows looking out of the Tower. Many were calling out of the windows for help and using the lights on their phones to attract attention. I could hear people calling up to them as well. I went to my phone to look up what was going on and started to pray that those who were in there would get out alive, because at this stage I couldn't tell that people were stuck. I suppose I was still hoping that everybody would just be able to get down the fire escape and get out all right, and of course what I had seen was so shocking that it only started to sink in very slowly.

I looked at my phone to see if it was already on the news, to see if there was an official story, but at this point it was just local people on social networking sites like me saying, 'Oh my goodness, look at Grenfell Tower, the whole thing is on fire, what on earth is going on here?' It was clear the Fire Brigade was already present and doing what they could, but it started to sink in that a huge tragedy was unfolding and that the fire was unstoppable.

I then posted a message to anyone who was reading my feed in the middle of the night, asking people to pray for those still in the Tower and that everyone could get out safely. There are evidently a lot of people on social media in the middle of the night, and right away some started responding to say they were praying.

I sat down for a few minutes and prayed. But then I started to think that I should go out there and try to be available to help. I didn't really know what I could do but I thought I might be able to help practically or offer to pray for people who were distressed, or something like that. I got dressed and put on a clerical shirt and dog collar and woke Gaby to tell her what was going on and to tell her that I was going out.

Crowds of local people had already started to form and a police cordon had been put in place. Some wanted to get into the building to go and help their loved ones. Many were on mobile phones speaking to people still trapped in the Tower, and the police officers manning the cordon were taking details. If you were speaking to someone inside and knew they were still alive, you passed their flat number to the police and they passed the details on to the Fire Brigade so that they could target flats that they knew had people still in them. I stood in the street, praying. At this point Gaby texted me to say she had not been able to get through to our friends who lived in the Tower, so we prayed that somehow they had got out.

One of the grimmest aspects of the unfolding disaster was that people could talk to their loved ones by phone but by then it was clear that it was very hard to get out. People were trapped. I realized I should wake Father Alan

Everett, the Church of England vicar in whose parish the Tower stood. I tried ringing him, and then walked to his house, rang his doorbell and explained what was happening. He got dressed, picked up his keys, and we went out together. Now there were two of us.

We opened St Clement's Church, which is just a few hundred metres away from the Tower, so that people who wanted could come in and say a prayer.

We then decided to try and find the muster point where people who had been evacuated were gathered. We thought we could go and offer support. We walked round the perimeter, and people told us various places were being used as gathering points but we couldn't actually find one. Even the police didn't seem to know where to point people towards. This was the first inkling that perhaps there wasn't a very coordinated response to the fire.

We returned to the church. I put the tea urn on. Father Alan lit some candles on the altar as a sign of prayer. Very quickly people started to come in, first a tiny trickle, then more as word spread that the church had been opened. When people arrived we offered them a hot drink and many were very grateful to be able to use the toilet.

One of the first to arrive was a firefighter. He came in very briefly, knelt to pray for a minute and then went back out again into the fray. I found that incredibly moving. If he had found just a moment of peace and strength in the midst of what he was doing and the terrible things he must have seen, then what we were doing was worth it for that alone.

As the night wore on, more firefighters came in to use the toilet and some of them chatted briefly. We thanked them for what they were doing and some brought unexpected encouragement, recounting how they were still rescuing people. Even quite late into the morning people were still being rescued, against expectations. Obviously, we had no idea what the casualty toll was going to be: rumours were flying around that hundreds were dead and hardly anyone was coming out alive. But the firefighters insisted, 'Don't give up hope yet!' We prayed the more fervently that others would be found alive and brought out.

From about 3 a.m. volunteers started coming in. As the local area woke up and more and more people realized what was happening, the church became a focal point for those who wanted to help as well as for those who needed help. Some volunteers were church members but there were a lot of other local people who just turned up to help too. By then, the low-rise blocks of flats at the base of the Tower had been evacuated because of fears that the Tower might collapse. That possibility was obviously terrifying for those residents, and for us, because we weren't far away. We recalled the 9/11 terrorism attack in the USA and remembered the way in which the Twin Towers simply collapsed. Thankfully that didn't happen in the case of Grenfell.

Because of the evacuation, over the early hours of the morning a lot of people started to take refuge in the church. There were parents with small children, families who had escaped without nappies or baby formula, people who had rushed out without bringing their medication with them. A sign of hope even in the midst of what was unfolding was the way in which so many people arrived to help, including doctors and nurses who just came in and offered their time voluntarily. That enabled people who needed medical assistance to receive it but also those who hadn't brought their medication with them to get prescriptions. I just kept making tea!

Quite early in the night people started arriving with supplies. I remembered listening to the missionary Heidi Baker talk about God's amazing provision in Africa, and how she and her co-workers never ask for money or resources but God always provides. The night of the fire really felt like that for me. We were obviously getting through a lot of cups, milk, tea and so on. Every time we noticed we were running out of something, someone would turn up and bring what we needed. A lady arrived with some paper cups just as we were running out of them. 'I happened to have some cups and I thought you might need these!' she explained.

A group of Muslims from east London had been awake late because it was Ramadan, and had seen what was happening on the news. They swiftly organized a huge response, bringing vans full of blankets, clothes, bottled water, snacks and toys for the children. I have no idea where their supplies came from, or how they gathered them so fast, but they were much appreciated. One of their group would ask me what else we needed and I would tell him; he then got on the phone to others and they somehow procured what we asked for in the middle of the night and brought it along – although as the days went on, many of the churches and other organizations in the community became totally overwhelmed with the volume of donations which had been sent in from all over the country. This was such a touching sign of people's compassion and desire to help those affected by the disaster, although it presented a lot of logistical challenges and indeed proved controversial locally when the Red Cross was asked to take the donations to sell them and *use* the money to help people affected – many local people felt that the money should be given directly to those affected by the fire and in particular to former residents of the Tower.

A local Muslim man started helping me and other volunteers to serve hot drinks and snacks. He was obviously fasting for Ramadan so he couldn't eat or drink himself. Later in the morning I left but he was still there serving. When I came back an hour or so later he was still there. I went away in the afternoon to have a nap as I was completely exhausted. I returned later that evening and he was *still* there. I asked if he had had any sleep and he said no, he had just popped home for a shower and then come back to keep helping. All of this without any food and water – his endurance and compassion were such an example and a sign of hope, as well as the way people of different religions and none were working alongside each other. Nobody had planned a multifaith or interfaith initiative – it was just that our common humanity prompted us all to respond to the tragedy. Later that evening, the church hosted an Iftar meal – the evening meal that breaks the Ramadan fast – in which people from across the community came and ate together.

A lot of that first night and early morning is a blur – I can't quite remember when particular things happened. At some point, staff arrived from the Tenant Management Organisation (or TMO – the body responsible for the Grenfell Tower on behalf of the Borough Council). They were trying to take details of people who needed temporary accommodation. We asked what was going on, what would happen now, where people would be taken. But there didn't seem to be a clear plan, and many were simply arranging somewhere to stay nearby with family or friends. Yet all morning we had been overwhelmed by people coming into the church and offering to accommodate individuals and families in their homes, and similar offers came in on social media as well. Officers from the TMO were logging the details, but hardly any of these offers were ever taken up. This gave us a taste of what became so clear later on, namely that the official response to the disaster was poorly coordinated and inadequate.

In contrast, we were simply offering a shelter, being there alongside people and meeting their most basic needs in terms of toilet facilities and cups of tea. People kept thanking us, but given the scale of the disaster, we didn't feel we were doing that much. We would have loved to have been able to do more. But doing what we could seemed to mean a lot. People wanted to be together: many didn't want to go off and find somewhere to stay and be on their own, or to go to work or school. Folk wanted to stay together, needing to be with others.

Another aspect of that night was that Father Alan and I were visible as local priests. The reason I was on the scene so quickly is simply that I live in this community – it is my home, not just a job. Similarly, Alan as the vicar also lives here all the time, so I was able to ring his doorbell in the middle of the night. The fact that we were wearing clerical collars and therefore were obviously priests also seemed to matter, and people have often contrasted our presence with the seeming absence of people from the local Council.

In reality, there were a lot of people from the Council and the TMO present, as I have said. Indeed, one local councillor volunteered at the church from very early in the morning and was there almost every day thereafter, helping out. It's not as if they weren't there. It was that people didn't *know* they were there. Like the councillor who helped in the church, they needed to be out and about, talking to people, hearing their concerns, listening to and understanding their anger and pain. And that was one of the things that made people angry – it looked and felt as if the Council was remote and unconcerned, even if this assessment was not always fair. It exacerbated the (absolutely justified) anger felt about the fact that the residents of the Tower had repeatedly raised concerns about fire safety which had clearly not been taken seriously or adequately addressed.

You can't tell who is a councillor or TMO officer by just looking at a person. But as priests, we were visible. It seemed to say to people that the Church was here, standing with them, and the Church cares. Nothing in my training as a priest could ever have really prepared me for what happened, at least not emotionally and spiritually, but at the same time I knew what to do. My training and instincts did kick in and tell me that I needed to be out there. They told me that I needed to get the vicar because he is the person who is responsible for this community. I don't think the parish system is the be-all and end-all of ministry, but it was absolutely one of those times when it really means something that every single community and therefore every single person in the country has a Church of England priest who is concerned for them and responsible for their spiritual well-being, and has a church which is there for them.

Having said that, one of the other reasons that St Clement's as a church was able to respond so quickly and well to the disaster was that for many years it has run the ClementJames Centre, a fantastic educational charity and community centre that is well known in the local community. This meant two things. First, the church had earned and received trust from many local people over many years. Second, it had some infrastructure and resources to develop the initial compassion of meeting physical needs into something more, for example arranging the meeting between local people and the Prime Minister at 10 Downing Street several days later. Something that gave me hope therefore in the midst of the horror was the way the Church of England works, in terms of having people like Father Alan and me who live somewhere locally, embedded in the community, and who are therefore known and able to respond very quickly when something happens. Such local people are also part of something bigger; that is, the wider structures of the Church of England, which were able to support us and offer advocacy at a national level. Later I went to visit the school my children attend, at which I am a governor. By the time I came back to church, loads of other clergy had turned up to help. It meant so much to have colleagues and our bishop supporting us and bringing backup so that we didn't have to be on duty 24/7 (although at first it felt that way!) and so that we could be sustained for the long haul of responding when the initial response had slowed down.

We will never be the same again, because of what has happened. Writing this several months after the fire, it remains the case that I am still utterly saddened by what took place. The sadness that my family feels (particularly my youngest child) has only increased. I can rarely think about it without tears – and I think that is probably right and healthy. I don't want what has happened to harden my heart, but the price you pay is letting yourself feel the pain.

At the same time, there has been so much to thank God for and such a strong sense of God's presence *in* the pain. Knowing God is there doesn't necessarily diminish the loss or anger, nor should it. But it enables you to see beyond the sadness and anger, to see that even though they are so serious and overwhelming, they are not the whole story. In particular, the thing that will stay with me and which gives me hope every day is the way in which the community and people from further afield united so rapidly, and with simple compassion, to respond to the need they saw, and

the way in which this meant so much to those who had
been affected.

One of the other clergy who had arrived was Father James
Heard. This is his account:

My phone buzzed into action early on the morning of
Wednesday 14 June. I glanced at the screen: Grenfell
Tower, North Kensington, fire, many feared dead. This was
only a mile away from my parishes in central Kensington.

I was stunned and it took a little time for me to take on
the enormity of the tragedy, but it was very clear people
were suffering and in need of support, so I reorganized
my diary and went straight to St Clement's Church and
community centre, just a few minutes' walk from the
Tower. Gathered there were those who lived on the
periphery of the Tower, evacuated because of the danger
posed by the fire.

I was stunned by what I saw. In the middle of this
tragedy, the response of the local community, of those
of different faiths and none, was extraordinary. Doctors
and nurses came to volunteer; a RBKC [Royal Borough
of Kensington and Chelsea] housing help-point and a
'missing person' desk were set up; the Samaritans offered
a listening ear. Someone had even set up a 'phone
charging' desk. And filling the church were supplies of
food, water, bedding and an avalanche of clothes. All the
local supermarkets had contributed, as had many

individuals. Many people simply sat in silence, numbed with shock by what they had experienced. We set up a prayer room: a place of calm and peace amid the hustle and bustle of activity.

The deanery response was to ask local churches to gather between six and ten volunteers for two-hour slots. I signed up my church for the 9–11 p.m. slot for that first day and sent out an email to my community. In the following two hours I received over 30 calls, text messages and emails from people offering to volunteer. We arrived at 9 p.m. and immediately set about helping: serving an Iftar meal at 9.19 p.m. when the Ramadan fast ended, sorting through the mountain of clothes, shoes, toys. We arranged a makeshift foodbank, as well as preparing for the following day's breakfast.

At 10 p.m. a group of young Muslims from east London arrived after their Ramadan prayers with a huge vanload to add to the collection of clothes, bedding, food, water, nappies, toiletries, even dog food. 'Dog food?' I questioned. Sure enough, five minutes later a resident came in with her dog, asking for dog food.

By 10.30 p.m. I was allowed through the cordoned-off area where, along with several priests, we spent time with members of the fire, police and ambulance services, obviously exhausted and many traumatized.

Father Peter Wolton, curate at our church, described his experience on that first night: 'The response really was amazing. People had come from across London and beyond; a family had driven from Croydon, another arrived from Harrow, a lady came from Derby and a retired couple of Red Cross volunteers from Horsham. A Sikh family needed to be housed and one had a health condition which meant Westway Sports Centre was unsuitable. I put them in touch with the dedicated line at RBKC and within 20 minutes they told me a solution had been found.'

One lady I met described her surprise when seeing a group of young teenage boys – usually on their bikes and looking rather intimidating – parking their bikes and asking how they could help. I put them to work sorting out clothes. 'It's not very glamorous work but it's really important,' I told them. A man came in with his piggy bank: 'I've been saving up for my summer holiday,' he said, 'but felt I had to help. Here it is; it's about £500.'

This support continued in the following days. Available the whole time were drinks, as well as halal, vegan and other food. I took a break one lunchtime to have some and was rather stunned by the quality of such large quantities of food. One of the volunteers told me, 'Oh, that was prepared by Stella McCartney's chef. And we have a team from a Jamie Oliver restaurant cooking supper this evening!'

The Bishop of Kensington encouraged clergy to be present and available to chat to people in the area around the Tower. I met one lady who had paused on her bicycle with the blackened Tower in view, smoke still bellowing. She was sobbing. She described how she remembered seeing the Tower being built in 1974 and had friends there, unaccounted for. She had been given the chance to purchase her council home, near the Tower, which she did. 'But it could easily have been in that Tower,' she said.

The Revd Gabby Thomas describes her experience: 'As I wandered about, locals grabbed my arm, often accompanied by the words, "Excuse me, vicar", and began to share stories and ask me what church I was from. One man whose friend had died in the fire wanted to show me the photographs he had taken of his harrowing night . . . Another friend joined him and began to tell me about the sound of bodies falling from the Tower, and how one man had fallen to the ground under the weight of catching a baby from a great height.'

Along with other clergy from across London, we stopped and listened to these harrowing stories with little other response than simply to share tears together.

A week on, the community gathered for an interfaith gathering in solidarity with the victims and survivors of Grenfell Tower. A Sikh representative spoke movingly, expressing that grief has no colour, creed, nationality, gender or background.

Another clergy person involved during and after the fire was the Rt Revd Graham Tomlin, Bishop of Kensington. I have

known and respected Graham for many years, since he interviewed me for theological college in 2003 and then subsequently went on to employ Sean at St Mellitus, the Anglican
theological college that he helped to found. Bishop Graham
recalls:

> I first heard of the fire when I saw a social media message
> on my phone at 6 a.m. on 14 June, asking for a comment.
> I had to work out which parish the Tower was located
> in, and very quickly rang Alan Everett, the vicar of the
> parish, to find out what was going on. I decided to drop
> everything that day and head up to North Kensington to
> do what I could to support the local church in its response
> to the fire.
>
> The Tower was still smoking when I arrived in the area.
> I visited St Clement's, which was full of local residents
> who had been evacuated from their homes, many in
> various states of confusion and anxiety, and an increasing
> pile of clothes, water bottles, food – donations of various
> kinds that were beginning to arrive. There were volunteers,
> police, media people and a lot of confusion!
>
> I rang the Police Borough Commander to ask if I could
> help in any way. She asked if I could gather some people
> to be around to talk to some of the firefighters who were
> going in and out of the building. I contacted a couple of
> local clergy, and we were allowed into the inner perimeter
> around the building, and spoke with the firefighters as

they recovered from their efforts, or prepared to go back in.

A couple of days later, I realized that many local people simply needed to talk. So I sent an email to all our clergy in the area suggesting that if they had the time and were willing to do so, they put on their clerical collar and simply walk the streets around the Lancaster West estate, getting into conversations as they happened. Many of them found themselves praying with people, offering blessings, counselling and pastoring people who needed someone to talk to.

We hastily arranged a service for local people at St Peter's Notting Hill on Friday, which I think was a helpful way to process people's thoughts, fears and hopes. On the Friday morning I received a phone call from number 10 Downing Street, asking if I could convene a group of local people to meet with the Prime Minister. With the help of St Clement's Church, and the ClementJames Centre, we brought together a group of local residents, survivors from the Tower, volunteers etc., and I chaired a meeting which enabled them to voice their concerns and perspectives to the PM [Prime Minister Theresa May]. The meeting was cut short, and continued the following day in Downing Street; I think it helped open up a conversation between the local community and the PM, which led to some initial response that was directed more to where people needed help. I also ended up doing quite a few media interviews, trying to describe to a wider audience what was happening on the ground, and trying to support local clergy as much as I could.

Bishop Graham was in fact in high demand for press interviews and stayed late helping people both in his role as Bishop but also in his role as a priest. He also attended many community meetings where he wisely did not speak but was there to support local people and clergy who were at the centre of everything that was happening.

I asked the Bishop if he could see anything to be hopeful about and he said:

I think in those first few days after the fire, we saw a little glimpse of what London and our wider community could be like. People were doing everything they could to try to help. They were volunteering, giving their clothes, money, food, anything they could to support others. Too often our life together is marked by competition, fear and self-centredness, but for a few days we suddenly saw a community that was centred upon helping each other, and that gives a little bit of hope for the future.

A young boy called Alfie came up to me on the Sunday morning following the fire – he came from Hounslow, and must have been around six years old. He had collected all his pocket money in a tin, and his dad told me that he wanted to give the money to the people who are affected by the fire. I took the money from him and promised I would deliver it. I gave it to the staff at the ClementJames Centre, who then passed it on to one of the families directly affected. It was perhaps a small picture of the outpouring of compassion and care from the wider community.

When I asked Bishop Graham what he thought was the way forward in order to encourage healing for the community, he responded with this:

It will be very difficult, but trust has to somehow be rebuilt between the local community and those in authority, whether the Council, the Government or others. I'm aware that it's hard to trust when you have felt betrayed, but no society can live without trust, and somehow that has to be rebuilt. That might happen only through the telling of stories, so that people really can understand one another and what their experience of life is in this part of London. It will take a long time, but needs to be done. In addition, we need to bring different communities together. Part of the problem that Grenfell revealed was the huge gap between the lives of the relatively wealthy in South Kensington, and the very different community in North Kensington – communities that had very little to do with one another. We somehow need to bring these communities together, in the kind of spirit that we saw in those first few days after the fire, but in a longer-term manner.

This is a task that only God can enable! Trust was shattered well before the fire, with the fire only highlighting why the community did not trust the authorities and in many cases why some people will always struggle to do so. Yet God is omnipotent. As his followers pray and seek reconciliation he can do marvellous things, and in such an awesome area where people have tasted community cohesion, perhaps they will long for more.

4

Urban hope

And who knows but that you have come to your royal position
for such a time as this?

(Esther 4.14b)

A surprising election result and a massive fire are very dramatic ways to begin, but the real start to our part of the story
is more prosaic.

Picture some beautiful new shoes. They might be a bit
uncomfortable at first, but as you wear them for a few days
you get used to them, and as time wears on they become your
favourite pair. Eventually you can't imagine wearing any
others. This is how I feel about where I live. It would not
perhaps be most people's first choice of location. Nor would
some of the previous homes I have had. This familiar old
shoe is actually where I want to stay, despite the harrowing
recent events.

Living in inner-city London is something I am very used to
now, but it wasn't where I started life. I was born a farmer's
granddaughter and lived from the ages of 5 to 18 on a farm in
rural Somerset with the nearest shops three miles away. My
experience of life was limited to the West Country and I had
no desire to stray too far from home.

But when I committed my life to Jesus, this all changed. I decided I would go anywhere and do anything he wanted me to do because I was in love with him, and as far as I could see, his plans were the best.

After university my faith led me to volunteer in Nottingham in an Urban Priority Area. Urban Priority Areas (UPAs) are unloved, unwanted and unwelcome in most cities. There is much awesome work being done in these places to show love and care for those who live there, but many there have been maligned. They are given names like 'chavs' to describe them because of the clothes they wear or the accents they have or even the way they like to decorate their homes. Yet these are people whom Jesus loves just as much as you or me.

I discovered that 80 per cent of Christians live in the suburbs and 20 per cent live in poorer areas. Also, 80 per cent of people live in these poorer districts and only 20 per cent in the suburbs. Christians are generally prosperous and live in richer places. Those who long to reach their community for Jesus are often doing it in the nice areas where people aren't afraid to go out at night, where there are no postcode wars or piles of litter on the streets. Where there is no overcrowding or poor housing.

I was convicted by my experiences and encouraged by hearing a man called Andy Hawthorne. As he preached I realized I didn't want a cosy life. I wanted to make a difference, to make my life count among the last, the least and the lost. Jesus frequented the places where people struggled; Jesus was to be seen speaking to those no one else would befriend, and some of them would probably have worn the biblical equivalent of shell suits, orange tans or imitation designer handbags.

The Bible talks about good news for the poor. Who could be poorer than those society has turned its back on? To some, that sounds like a nightmare, but to me it sounded like a calling!

I decided I wanted to live in the inner city, in the tough places. If people warned me not to live somewhere, that was usually the place I needed to go. When my husband asked me to pray about being his girlfriend (honestly, he really did!), I was living on a settled traveller estate. I told him I would only go out with him if he accepted that, if we ever got married, I only ever wanted to live in Urban Priority Areas, those places least loved, least cared for. He agreed to my request, so I agreed to his!

My decision presented some challenges. I remember one incident when local youths broke the glass in my front door. Some friends came to help me mend the hole. One was furious when he left his saw propped outside the house for a few moments only to discover it had been stolen while he was inside. It was going to be tough persuading people that this was a call from God!

When my husband and I went to theological college and married a couple of years later, we specifically chose only to accept placements in UPAs. That is harder than it sounds when you live in Oxford.

We sensed God calling us to London, although I was confused by this call because I never realized multiculturalism was my thing. I felt guilty about it, but I was actively scared of people of other faiths, especially Muslims. I had met very few, and didn't know what it would be like to live around people who believed in a different God.

We worked for three years in an amazing multicultural church, St Gabriel's Church in Cricklewood, north-west London, where we made many cultural errors and were gently educated by the people who had been there since racism was the norm. They helped us learn what is culturally appropriate. I was also privileged to make friends with people of other faiths, especially the Muslims of whom I had been so scared.

After this it was time to move on and we sensed a new calling to west London. We weren't sure where exactly, but we were using the Trellick Tower in Kensington as our guide. We also looked at what Eden – a movement that sends Christian missionaries out to live their faith in the toughest areas of the world – was setting up in west London. The group was starting three projects, and we were torn. We felt very strongly that we were called to live in one area, but called to worship in a different Eden area. Up to this point I had not been sure of the reason. We worship in Dalgarno Way, but we live here, in the shadow of Grenfell Tower. This fact has filled us with pain but also brought our calling into focus.

As we prayed and deliberated, a friend, Steve, who drove a taxi, confirmed the call for us. He was driving down Silchester Road when he saw in his mind's eye Sean's name on the side of a block of flats. This block was the very one we were debating about living in. It was the only flat in our budget in the whole area, but it was on the third floor with no lift, while we had two tiny children and hoped to have more. This word confirmed it to us, all the same, and we put the deposit down and moved in the following week.

A year later, in September 2011, when I was 35 weeks pregnant with our third child, we moved across the road to Waynflete Square, which has been our home ever since. I have always loved the cityscape view of the towers and flats surrounding us. At night it has always been particularly beautiful, a far cry from the fields of Somerset where I was raised, but no less lovely.

Both our flats have allowed us clear views of Grenfell Tower. I would often wake in the middle of the night in our first local home and see lights on all over the Tower at odd times, and would wonder who was up and what they were doing. Now the Tower is dark during the day and dark at night. I find it a very uncomfortable sight, and many others tell me they can't even look at it. Not everyone feels that way. Jimmy Bracher has lived here all his life. He observes:

A lot of people are saying they should knock it down. I kind of like having it there. I'll miss it. Even the burnt-out hulk it is now. I'll still be really disappointed when it's gone. I understand folk don't want a reminder, but I want to remember, even though it was a terrible fire. It will be really weird not having Grenfell Tower there.

Grenfell is quite iconic for this area for many reasons. It has always had a group of residents who were united and prepared to stand up for their safety and the common good. Although there are lots of residents' associations, the Grenfell Action Group has always been particularly vocal. None of the other blocks seemed to have quite as much motivation or organization to see what they needed and request it.

I first came into contact with the Grenfell Action Group at a public meeting about a proposed new academy, not long after we first arrived in the area. I expected to attend a pleasant meeting full of hope and excitement about the proposals to turn an old car park and a couple of football pitches into a secondary school, with a new sports centre thrown in. I'd used the park below the Tower and counted at least five different secondary school uniforms, and realized the families in the Tower and other local residents needed a school in the area. There are five local primaries so clearly a secondary school was necessary.

When I arrived for the meeting, I realized my expectations were completely wrong. I saw people lobbying outside and waving petitions around. It turned into a big fight between the Council and the local residents, many of whom did not want a secondary school on their patch. In truth, the area had been under siege from developers for so long that they had learned to petition for their rights, and their trust of official figures was so low that any change to the neighbourhood was unwelcome.

The disagreement continued. Eventually the Council committed to making the building project as low key as possible, to be as considerate as possible and to make as many improvements as they could to Grenfell Tower. They also committed to keeping trees in the middle of the site.

The project unfolded and the plans for the school mushroomed into a reality. However, the power of the people inside Grenfell Tower was clear. They were frustrated by the way they were treated and they weren't going to be quiet until they got what they wanted, or at least the best version of plan B! Thus started many months of work on the building. The Council added cladding to the exterior to make it look like a white rocket, and put in new kitchens and bathrooms. The crèche and boxing gym were completely transformed, and the whole site now looked ready for a fresh new future with school, sports centre – and a sparkling Grenfell Tower. How little we knew! The upheaval in the local community was mainly created by the noise and mess of building work, but also by the fact that the old sports centre had to close. We were told it was closing in September, but it remained open until December, with all the staff being kept in the dark about what was happening and when.

The school was officially opened by Her Royal Highness the Duchess of Cambridge on Monday, 19 January 2015, but had already been operational since September 2014. The sports centre opened in March 2015, and I and my friends were part of one of the first baby swimming classes. The impact of the building work had been great, but at the time it felt worth it for the prize of receiving a brand-new school and sports centre – and we were going to enjoy it.

The Kensington Leisure Centre (the sports centre) was central to my life from the start. When my little girl Esther was one year old we joined her first parent-and-toddler swimming class. She took to water like a seal and would regularly scare the other parents and lifeguards by taking running jumps into the teaching pool. One quick-witted parent once managed to catch her by her swimsuit straps as she launched herself into the air! She always bobbed back to the surface with a massive grin on her face, to choruses of 'Gosh, she's brave!' The swimming class was eclectic and had mums, dads and nannies within it from a huge range of socio-economic groups. We became a friendly, welcoming bunch, and regularly had coffee together after the class. Most of my friendships now are based around that class and the parents I met there. We developed from swimming buddies to friends. Many of us frequent the leisure centre several times a week, ostensibly for our kids alone! There is also a cheerful day-spa upstairs and a large sports hall where we pretend to play badminton on a weekly basis.

Grenfell Tower and its surroundings, and the school and sports centre, quickly became quite a campus for us. The community uses the school for extracurricular activities, and the school, sports centre and Grenfell formed three sides of a triangle, all facing on to a small pink climbing frame (or 'statue'). From the school you could clearly see the Tower and leisure centre. The green space was used for exercising dogs and children, and the paths all interconnected so that whichever way you wanted to go through this campus, there was a path in that direction.

As a Christian who is keen to share the love of God, I have prayed and walked around that area many times. I have also stopped and chatted to friends whom I meet there in the crossroads of our lives outside the Tower. Gradually I became familiar with the people who lived in the Tower itself. There was little anonymity for them as their entrance was completely overlooked by other people's homes. That perhaps is why we as a community feel we knew these people so well and why, as their beautiful faces were printed on to posters and stuck to our walls, fences and memory walks, the sight was so poignant for us all.

One memorable time my smallest son, Caleb, was trailing behind us and then, unbeknown to me, dashed off to play on the pink statue. I was taking a slightly different route home and Esther was walking along a low wall painfully slowly. I turned around to repeat the frequent cry, 'Come on, Caleb!' – and suddenly he was nowhere to be seen. I called the older children back and we started a fruitless search down each of the pathways from the crossroads. I alerted the leisure centre and within two minutes they had three people out combing the area. A friend searched the whole building, and another friend dashed home to get his bike and scour the local streets.

Spotting a large group of ladies in hijabs talking together, I approached them with tears in my eyes, asking if anyone had seen my son. Within seconds these generous women divided themselves into four teams and each took a path.

By this point Caleb had been gone for 25 minutes and my calm demeanour was cracking. I called the police and as I was speaking to them one of the ladies returned with news. Caleb had made it most of the way home alone and a newspaper distributor had seen him in tears. One of our lovely Somalian lady friends, who lived in a tower behind our flat, had found him and was trying to find us to return him. As no one was home she took him to where she had last seen us, and where my husband – who was by this point on his bike roving the streets – finally found them.

This incident made me aware of how grateful I was for the community I live in, where I can know and be known. It doesn't take much, just time spent in the local park where the children play together, a cheery wave and a greeting to the lady also struggling to get her four kids to school. On the strength of that, she recognized my son and was able to help him. Many of those women who split into teams lived in Grenfell Tower. One of them died in the fire with her family. I recognized her from her picture. She helped my son, but even my most fervent prayers could not help her.

I had been afraid of these people who spoke a different language and prayed in a different way to a God I did not recognize. They have become my friends, my neighbours, and people whom I love and need. We're not in Somerset any more, but it is a privilege to share some of my life and rural upbringing as they share their lives with me.

For each of us our pilgrimage looks different and this has been mine. My faith has been walked out, lived and loved for the past few years on these streets and paths, swum through and chatted through. I don't claim to have led anyone to Jesus, but my hope and prayer is that my friends and neighbours will turn their heads towards him because they know me, and that in his great power and mercy he will draw them into himself.

This is my mission field and I have been blessed enough to share it with several amazing Christians. God has called some really great people here. There are the long-timers at the Latymer Community Church: Jackie, Simon, Mary and Derek. These people have loved, prayed, given, shared and lived out their faith for several decades. Each of them has a strong sense of calling and a 'hand to the plough' attitude. There has been little fruit, in terms of the size of our churches, but they are very loving, and they have faithfully served the community in the power of Jesus.

There are other fantastic Christians up on the Portobello, such as the Salvation Army and Notting Hill Community Church, who just keep going, often in very difficult circumstances. There are the lovely Anglican churches with their wide-ranging practices and theology, offering everything from weekly mass to Bible study groups, and Notting Hill Methodist Church, which has also been a key part of the story since the fire.

My particular friends are the Eden team, people who were called by God to live here at around the same time as me. These guys have poured their lives into this area. It has often been tough. They have worked with gang members, with the plentiful 'not yet Christians', and continue to do amazing work, especially with the girls, despite enormous challenges. They have seen some of the community's young people die or go off the rails and they have gone on loving them.

God has sent people from all over the UK and the world to serve in this area, and he has a plan. We may not be from around here originally, but this has become our home and we are claiming this territory for God. The devil wants to ruin and wreck our every venture, but we keep going because we know the God who wins in the end.

Did God send us here for such a time as this? The Esther passage at the start of this chapter has been hung on my daughter Esther's wall since well before the fire. She has always been someone who lives up to her name, Esther Joy Elizabeth. Esther means 'little star', and she has always been early to walk, talk and generally formulate opinions beyond her years. She was named for the character in the Bible, and in our family we joke that she was born to rule, like Queen Esther. However, the verse now holds meaning for our whole family: 'And who knows but that you have come to your royal position for such a time as this?' (Esther 4.14b).

In order to help us understand this verse let me turn to John 1.12–13:

Yet to all who did receive him, to those who believed in his name, he gave the right to become children of God – children born not of natural descent, nor of human decision or a husband's will, but born of God.

John tells us that those who believe in the name of Jesus are part of God's family. Revelation 19.16 tells us that God is the King of Kings and the Lord of Lords. By becoming a Christian I joined the family of this High King. If we are made sons and daughters of the King, we are princesses and princes in the kingdom of God. We are now royalty, not because of anything we have done, but because of what God has done through us and for us in Jesus.

The Esther verse suggests that we may have come to our 'royal position' or, as we understand it in our context, to faith in Christ, for such a time as this. What an awesome thing! Perhaps Sean and I became Christians for such a time as this? We were not the only Christians who felt that. Father Alan Everett, a local Anglican priest and our friend, described his response after leaving his house and opening the church doors at 3 a.m. as a refuge during the fire. 'Those two actions, that one moment, feels like the core, the heart, of my entire ministry as a priest,' he said.

The seven years we were here before the fire were gorgeous times of making friends, having babies and rooting ourselves in the school and community. What does it mean if actually this is the thing for which we are here? What if this was part of God's big plan for our lives?

I felt there was definitely a purpose for my life and I have never wavered from this. When I became a Christian and started to try to serve God, I continued to believe in this purpose, never being totally sure of what it was but not doubting its existence.

As I found a call to live in the inner city, I found more purpose; as I prayed and found what I believe was God's choice of husband for me, I found more; as we had the ideal number of children for us, I knew this was all God's purpose. Esther was most certainly God's plan for us, as it is through her we have made so many friends and really dug our roots into the neighbourhood.

Esther is very vivacious and chatty and as I am an introvert who likes a bit of peace and quiet, Esther and her 24/7 'talkingness' (as she terms it) proved quite a challenge. I felt as if God had something else for her and I needed a break.

None of our three older children went to nursery until they were at least three and a quarter. I have no idea why I picked the lovely but costly option of sending her to St Peter's, a Christian nursery, but it seemed like the right thing to do and miraculously all the money always came in to pay for it despite fees that seemed well above our means. There was no special reason I felt more led there than anywhere else; I just had it in my head that that was where Esther should go. So she did.

The nursery, however, is where she met her good friend Amaya and her gorgeous, kind and generous family. As a busy mum of four, knowing she would only attend that school for one year, I didn't seek to make too many friends among the parents. Nevertheless this one family took us under their wing. They lived in Grenfell Tower itself, just around the corner from us, and so it was convenient to go there for the children to play, and we would also often see them about. Esther and Amaya played nicely together, and we were invited to her birthday party and she came to Esther's.

I never spoke to Amaya's family about faith, except to learn they were Muslim but not particularly adherent. Esther just chatted her way through nursery. Amaya's parents always spoke of how she talked about Esther, and they were pleased that she was helping Amaya to learn good English. Esther's purpose at the age of two was to make a lovely friend.

If I had known ahead of time that this friendship would have been so tragic, would I have changed my choice of nursery? Would I have turned down the family's kind hospitality? No, I don't believe I would. Esther has been profoundly affected by the death of her friend and this is something no three-year-old should have to face, but I believe God's purpose was behind our friendship and our location.

I don't believe God caused the fire, but I do believe he put his people into places such as this for such a time as this. To be part of a grieving community where you hold the words of hope and eternal life and can offer them to people is a powerful gift, and a powerful purpose.

Amaya came to Esther's third birthday bearing a card with Disney princesses all over it. When I found this card after the fire, I wept. It says: 'Get ready to dream big . . . you're 3'. Her parents had dreams for her to learn, to grow and flourish. We all have these dreams for our children.

Their dreams ended that terrible night in the smoke and flames. Their extended family's dream ended too and we were left wondering why they should die in this way.

Jesus came so we could have life and live it to the full (John 10.10). How does this sad story connect with this scripture? It's an exhortation to live your life to the full, to do and be all God has called you to be, because life may be short. Every day counts.

We truly had no idea why we were called here nor what we had to do. We have seen little fruit other than some amazing friendships and we now feel like part of the furniture. It's our 'hood'! We are trying to live life to the full here. In both moving here and sending Esther to St Peter's we were trying to follow our calling. What did God have for us? How can we bless him by living out our normal lives? These were just two of many decisions we made towards living out life in all its fullness.

Now we see why. If we hadn't sent our daughter to that nursery, she would never have met her friend. We would never have met the family. They would just be tragic faces on a poster to us.

I don't know whether Amaya and her family knew Jesus. I know she would have been introduced to him at the Christian nursery and she may have become his friend. She was best friends with several children who were best friends with Jesus and who all had their purpose to love her. What I do know is that when I prayed for some sign from God about this, I met a mutual friend and she told me her five-year-old son had had a dream. In this dream he saw Amaya. He gave her a hug and then she said to him, 'I have to go now and be with God.' God knows what we need and he holds the answers to our deep questions. This dream may be just a dream, but perhaps it is the peaceful message I needed to hear from the King.

There are times when I am doing 'the right thing' and it's tough. Today I took the kids to the library, to the doctor's and to the shops. They were keen to take the car to drive the half mile but I insisted on dragging them there on foot. It's not very far and even the three-year-old can manage it; and it's good for us all to get a bit of exercise and not burn up the planet with a tiny journey. I am blessed to have the choice, although they did repeatedly suggest the bus was also a good option! Walking home got slower and slower, and by the end I was nearly on my knees with frustration, as was my eldest daughter. The little ones, easily distracted, drove us wild by stopping to touch everything and by keeping to a snail's pace. However, I maintain that I am doing the right thing by my children even it isn't what suits them or what is easiest. Character lessons are only learned through taking the right, sometimes tough, path. No one ever built good character by taking the easy way out repeatedly and that's something I want them to learn.

In the same way, the things that God calls us to do are often very hard. He wants us to grow into his image and he is the image of love, so unless we too are the image of love laid out in 1 Corinthians 13 – the love that is patient and kind – we are due for some challenges. If every time things look a bit ugly we withdraw, we are going to miss out on some of the best formation we can get.

Sometimes it's tempting to throw in the towel and move to Somerset. The house prices are more affordable and the air is beautifully clean. We have family in that county, and there is so much space for the kids to roam around and they can have a different type of freedom, the freedom I grew up with, where the only ones noticing your misdemeanours are the rabbits in the fields. However, there is something so beautiful and compelling about being in the place where you know God wants you to be. I have friends who doubt their abilities and wonder if they are living in the right place, or if they have the right friends, or if their kids are in the right schools or have the right future mapped out. I stopped worrying a few years ago because, as a friend once pointed out, almost none of the things she worries about ever happen. I feel that I was sent by God to live where I do and that even horrible tragedy shouldn't dissuade me. This is when God is going to show his strength, when I am at my weakest.

I feel as if many of the things I have been praying for have been happening since the fire. That is why I wanted to write a book that stressed there was hope. The Grenfell tragedy was the worst thing I have ever seen, yet I believe that the God who made all things can make good happen out of bad. I believe he can draw people to himself despite their pain and suffering, and I have seen so much to praise him for in the aftermath. Let me share my stories and see if you agree.

5

Hands off, it's ours!

There are issues with living on council estates, in property owned by a large corporation or social tenancy landlord. If there is a problem with your flat the owner or estate manager should try to right the wrong, but you may be job number 103 for the day and these things can often be forgotten. By the next day your job may be buried under a pile of paper, or overlooked entirely. People who get things done generally know the system; they learn to shout the loudest, insist the most frequently, or are articulate enough to find out who to speak to and how to speak to them.

The system is flawed and unjust, and this leads people to be dissatisfied and mistrustful of people in general. With language often a barrier, it becomes even harder to know whom to trust.

Imagine, if you will, the well-known Roald Dahl story, *Charlie and the Chocolate Factory*. Charlie, a poor boy whose parents can only afford to buy him one bar of chocolate a year, wins a ticket to visit an extraordinary chocolate factory. By the end of the visit he is given the factory as a gift by the eccentric owner, Mr Willy Wonka.

Imagine what it was like to be Charlie. He went from destitution and extreme poverty, with no one caring about him and his family, to a point where suddenly he was the centre of a media circus. There would have been a frenzy of interest in him. Picture that first day when he and his family moved into their new home and shut the door. The whole amazing world of sweets and chocolate was theirs for the taking. They had suffered and struggled for so long, and suddenly people cared and they had access to everything they needed. Not just the things that they had never had but wanted, like sweets, but all the other things too. Plentiful food, a warm bed, a roof that didn't leak, a position in the community and a secure future.

Now transfer this analogy to North Kensington. People in Lancaster West and Silchester and the other estates have struggled for years to be heard, to be understood, to be taken seriously. The community has been through a terrible time, with more tragedy than anyone should witness, and suddenly the eyes of the world are on it. The media frenzy, the interest in the community, the care and resources they were previously denied: all are now available – or so we hoped.

We thought things were going to get much better for local people, as it did for Charlie.

Counselling is now available all hours of the night and day. There is funding for projects that was previously unavailable. A local friend was working in a job partnering NHS and other organizations and was told that there was to be a gap between her project finishing and the start of a new one in a year's time. She would have been made redundant and then had to reapply for her job a year later. The funding has subsequently been found to bridge the gap between the two projects. This should always have been the case – for a health and well-being programme in a deprived area – but it took massive destruction for this to happen.

The public now want to hear our concerns. Television stations and newspapers are interested in our views.

There are amazing services locally, partly because of the slums that used to exist in this area. Long-standing charity work has been established. The Rugby Portobello Club offers a fantastic service, with youth clubs and facilities for mums and toddlers. It runs a place where clothes and toys and baby equipment are available for free. These are donated by the well-to-do for the less well-done-by, which gives rise to the local phenomenon of parents dressing their children in cast-off designer clothes. The Harrow Club is a similar project but mostly focuses on young people, while the ClementJames Centre is mainly concerned with local education and employment. The Harrow Club was set up by Harrow School, and the Rugby Club by Rugby School, while ClementJames is run by St Clement's Church. There was a lot of sharing and caring in the area before the fire, and these charities were centres where victims could go for help both during and after.

The advantages of living in this area have always been great. There is, for example, free full-time nursery care for our children in a local school, although government cuts will soon end this. It is very good for people who live here and want to work or just to have a bit of space from their little ones. This is subsidized by the school since nursery budgets have been slashed.

There are many aspects to living in North Kensington for which the local Council deserves credit. Nevertheless, there have been a large number of concerns. One has been the regeneration of the Silchester estate. For several years residents have been living under the shadow of the Council's plans to redevelop the whole of the Silchester area, to knock it down and start again. The different stages of planning and decision-making have been incredibly stressful. There have been many confusing options laid out (all of which included destroying my own home!), and several times a year residents have been invited to comment on the different possibilities.

We have commented. We have argued. We have marched; we have protested. We have fought this regeneration with planning meetings and petitions, silent vigils, noisy vigils and awkward questions. Many of the elderly people in my block have been worried about what might happen to them. Often they have lived in the same flat for 40 years, since the estate was built, and thought it would be their last home. The regeneration has led many of us to angry tears, frustrated sighs and panicked plans, and broadly three years of uncertainty and stress. People are not against more homes being built, but our experience of other local regeneration projects led us to believe that the new homes would be for the rich, and there wouldn't actually be more affordable homes built. People were also concerned that the replacement homes would be smaller and of lower quality and we would lose a lot of our green space just so that there could be a 'traditional street pattern', something that the Council has been planning for a few years.

Since the fire, the regeneration plans have been completely scrapped. After the council leaders stepped down, every regeneration plan was destroyed. This has been a sign of hope for us and a source of great relief. The final decision was due to be made in September 2017, and before August was over the plans had been axed. The battle we were fighting was one that we stood a very small chance of winning, but in the light of Grenfell our voices have actually been heard and our area is to be left in peace for now. Our pleas of 'Hands off, it's our area' have finally been heard!

The plans were a high-handed developer's dream. They included less play space, more high-rise blocks of flats, more commercial development and no private gardens. The flats were going to be a mix of social housing and privately owned homes. The private housing would probably have sold in the region of £450,000 for a one-bedroomed flat with a small balcony, replacing three-bedroom homes with gardens; the developers would buy the original homes under compulsory purchase also for about £450,000, so those who currently live mortgage-free (because they have already paid for their own homes) would have to remortgage in order to live in a property of a similar size to the one they previously occupied – and, to top it all, without the benefit of large balconies or gardens. Private tenants like us would have had to move out of the area altogether, with a chance of renting smaller properties at a later date. Our community would have been largely destroyed.

In the light of all our community has been through, the abandonment of this policy barely registered. Residents didn't have the energy to express their joy at the end of the battle because it came through such tragic circumstances and we were so weary. We remain suspicious that this initiative may yet re-emerge in a different form. I, however, choose to celebrate the fact that for now I can remain peacefully in my own home with space for my family, survivors from our own miniature war-zone.

This suspicious attitude may sound far-fetched. Why are people so 'up in arms'? The issue is that Grenfell is not the only tower block in our area. There are four others, nearly as tall, each with 19 floors, each less than 250 metres from Grenfell Tower. The majority of these blocks are run by the TMO, the same management structure that ran Grenfell, and the residents therefore have understandable safety concerns. There are also hundreds of people living in low-rise blocks who feel equally unsafe. In this community there are also very strong links between people of the same nationalities in the same way that any expatriate communities work. People who share culture and language connect without trying. So those in the high-rise blocks have a strong sense of solidarity, only enhanced by the fire.

After the fire, people needed to gather and discuss the way forward. These meetings offered members of the community a chance to voice their opinions and pain, and the idea was that the authorities would come in and listen. This should have been an ideal time for solidarity and bonds of friendship.

However, this is not quite the way the meetings went. Imagine a room full of scared, mistrustful people who don't know how to distinguish the goodies from the baddies. There are many wolves among the lambs, and no one knows who is who or what a person's agenda is.

These meetings – and there have been many – vary in their composition.

The key meetings have been for those who were actually resident in Grenfell Tower, who have suffered more than anyone. According to a respected local charity, approximately 255 escaped from the fire, about 80 of them actually rescued by firefighters. These people are the priority, the ones who most deserve justice. Everyone else pales into insignificance.

These poor people have also been the focus of media speculation. Journalists and social workers and council representatives have been chasing after these survivors for different reasons. Some are justifiable, such as creating new forms of ID and helping with accommodation. However, many of these primary survivors have been subjected to endless unwanted press attention, as well as exploitation by people who claim solidarity with them but are in fact pursuing their own agendas.

Then there are those who were evacuated because of the fire, in some cases because their homes lacked a supply of gas and hot water. They were rehoused in hotels, or stayed with friends or family. Most lived within a short step of the Tower and many want never to return to their previous homes – even if those homes are safe, clean and functional. Some had heard and seen things that were seared upon their memories, causing them to find sleep elusive and flashbacks frequent. For the most part these folks needed to carry on with normal life. Their kids came to school; the parents carried on working. Many were lodged in local hotels, which was fine for a night or two but not for weeks or even months on end. As time passed some were rehoused, while others drifted back to their former homes as the gas and hot water returned, but some were still living in hotels months afterwards with nowhere to go to and no way back, because their old residences were considered unsafe.

Then come people like us. We are locals. We have not had to move home and the inconveniences of the aftermath have been purely practical, such as roadblocks, an increased police presence and greater levels of noise and people on the streets. We may well know people who have died. We were probably woken by the sirens. Nearly all of us saw the fire. We are the sympathetic majority who are trying to help, to hold our shaken community together. We are able to benefit from the various kindnesses that people have offered, and most of us have been involved in the aftermath, sorting clothes or providing things people need. We have found ways to express our grief and solidarity: we have tied ribbons, gone on vigils and marches, and tried to carry on with our lives.

Many from outside the borough have also appeared at meetings, sometimes provoking suspicion and resentment from the locals. Some simply wanted to help, travelling from all over the UK. These people don't know anyone personally but they feel as if the Grenfell fire was their tragedy too. Many have given their time tirelessly and ceaselessly. They have joined our fluid community and walked with us. We have gradually learned to trust them.

Then there are the professionals: the police, the firefighters, the clergy, the imams. These people probably don't live locally but have some form of responsibility for the area. When life is going well, few appreciate what responsibilities these people hold, but when tragedy strikes we become all too aware of their roles. By and large these men and women have been welcomed.

Then come the council members and staff sent to represent the borough. These people may or may not live locally but they are generally not welcome! Many are well-meaning, but the years of high-handed conduct by North Kensington Council – above all, over the redevelopment plans – have sown deep-rooted mistrust.

The meetings generally started with someone from one of the professional groups making a report or sharing some news. They were then interrupted by questions from one set of locals or another. The questions were rarely answered, however, because others offered differing perspectives or disagreed with the professional. This was the general pattern for weeks on end. People on these different levels rarely saw eye to eye. Helpful information was circulated via a regular newsletter, but the community meetings generally descended into chaos and confusion. I attended one meeting where an elderly local gentleman pushed a lady. The community was effectively in pieces – but still we had to keep together, all painfully aware that this is our community and always will be, especially once we are no longer interesting to the media and politicians.

The problems have been compounded because those who previously ran the Residents' Associations and sat on the Tenant Management Organisations have been worn out by these meetings. Many are stepping down.

One good thing that has emerged from the meetings is that the Council, the police and all those who are trying to help, including the Church, have realized that this community is full of individuals. One size does not fit all. Some people want financial assistance; some want reassurance; others are desperate for mental health support and help for their children. Through the meetings many different voices have been heard.

I heard one young black man at a meeting say, 'After Grenfell I found my voice.' He is one of many who were previously silent, but this is what it took for him to learn how to express himself. After this, I saw him being interviewed on television and on YouTube. He wasn't the only one. I too found my voice and began to speak more loudly and constructively. Others were not afraid to speak out any more because they felt they had nothing left to lose. Those things that previously held people back no longer seemed to apply. Social niceties, fear, language barriers were all broken as residents tried to express their hurt and pain.

Kim Taylor-Smith, new deputy leader of the Council, said at one community meeting for Silchester residents, 'The book had been written on the second day. The Council let people down. I've got to write the second book.' He is right when he says a new book – a new narrative about this neighbourhood – needs to be written, but this is a book for us all to write: the story of how the community got back up again and built new hope, a new story of cohesion, peace and love rather than bitterness and blame. No matter who is to blame, forgiveness is going to be a key part of moving forward and healing for Grenfell.

As the news reports were coming in, they often called this area 'poor'. Even Ben Okri in his poem 'Grenfell Tower, June 2017' refers to the people in Grenfell as poor. This is not a title many of the local residents would have assigned to themselves. Yet if it does apply, why are they poor? In truth, they are poor because of the housing and conditions in which they and many others like them live. They are poor because they had to accept these homes or be made homeless, because that is how the housing policy works. They are poor because they don't have a choice. They are poor because their complaints about the safety of their building were not listened to and acted upon quickly enough. They are poor because they don't have the backstop of wealth.

If you lost your job tomorrow and couldn't get another, how long would it take for you to end up on the street? For some, connections would kick in and they'd ease their way into a new job. Others could go back home to Mum and Dad, knowing they are always welcome in hard times. Some might have good friends who would host and support them until they sorted themselves out. But others have nothing – no backstop, no family or at least not in the UK, no savings, no safety net.

As I read the reports and considered the implications of poverty, I realized that wealth means choice. Often laws don't apply to those with money, because they can pay someone to find a loophole big enough to fit through. Yet this community has something more powerful than wealth. It has spirit, and it has love.

Zaila, a local mum who has been posting regularly online about Grenfell, said this about the local area:

> The love and strength of the community, especially in those first couple of days/weeks, was awesome. It brought everyone together, whoever you were. If you witnessed Grenfell as it happened you were part of the community and it was something you could never walk away from.

This is, as she implies, a fluid community, one which people can join and be part of if they are respectful of the diversity of the area.

If you want to be in, you can be in. This isn't an exclusive group that you can't fit into because you are too black/white/ fat/thin/clever/stupid/honest/crooked. We are all 'too something' to be part of anything, yet here we are all fitting in together.

We work at it. We greet our neighbours. We tell people that the place where we live is great. We don't slate it. We say we are lucky to be living here. We believe our own press. We truly know we are blessed, although others looking in from the outside may judge us and not want to live in our supposedly small, shabby flats. They may be horrified at the lack of space we have and the dog muck on the streets and the overcrowding of our homes, yet we feel blessed. We live near royalty in Kensington Gardens. We may be poor but we are rich.

In the time after the fire, the love of the community was palpable. You couldn't see people you knew without asking them how they were. We shared depth and pain with relative strangers, because we were local. My children grew fed up with me stopping to talk to yet another person and find out how he or she was, but every individual was precious, someone we had not lost to the flames.

One day I came across a line in my daily Bible reading which offered me comfort: 'you are in our hearts, to die together and to live together' (2 Corinthians 7.3b ESV). This verse encapsulated for me what it meant to live in such a community.

How can a tragedy like this be turned into something positive? How can there be hope when the authorities have failed, the fire services are underfunded and so many people are dead or missing, while families have been wiped out and joy has turned to sadness in countless homes? Ecclesiastes 3.11 tells us that God makes 'everything beautiful in its time. He has also set eternity in the human heart; yet no one can fathom what

God has done from beginning to end.' God will never stop picking up this fallen world. Every time we fail or falter he is there, encouraging us, imploring us to get up and keep going. We may be tripping and stumbling, but God, the creator of the universe, keeps picking us up and carrying us forward, then gently placing us back on our feet when we are ready. We may no longer be able to stand. This pain may have crippled us, but someone else, somewhere close, has the strength to go on. Someone else has a kind word or a hug to share with me, and if I look I'll find that person.

Something that has struck me since the tragedy is that people greet you with the words, 'How are you?' And they actually mean it. They genuinely want to know how I am, and are prepared to ask further questions about my well-being. If I need love and support, all I have to do is ask.

I find that people who previously would offer no more than a casual 'hello' are now my good friends. I now greet with hugs and kisses people whom I previously only knew to smile at. Our children are friends, and we are sharing life in a way that a year ago I could only have dreamed of. I have prayed for this community for seven years now – that God would break in. I have prayed for opportunities to pray for my neighbours on the street, and finally this is happening.

In the week after Grenfell I prayed for two people I knew – on the street, in public. They were desperate; they needed God's help, and were prepared to receive it on the street! One had barely spoken to me previously, yet now we are friends. As we share our vulnerability and pain, we are strengthened by each other. We don't feel alone or isolated in this little island in London. We are part of a people. We are the survivors of a tragedy for which we were totally unprepared, yet we found strength by joining together. This is not a bond that can be easily forgotten.

In a way, this is also not something that can be replicated – but you can pray on the streets for your own neighbourhood! If, as you walk about your daily business, you ask God to bless the streets you live on and to help you share his love with your neighbours, you may be surprised at the results. What if the God who created everything actually cares about you and your neighbourhood? What if you didn't end up where you are because you happened to like the area, but actually because God wants to use you to share his love where you are?

God's mission is exciting. God's call is exciting. Secretly blessing people and praying around the local streets is exciting. Being given a mission to do what only you can do is phenomenally fun. In 1 Corinthians 3.9, the apostle Paul talks about us being co-workers with Christ. It's like going to do the gardening with a small child and a plastic spade. You tell her the patch of ground you want dug and she starts with her small spade and you with a large. When you've both finished she feels a sense of achievement in the same way we do when working with God. He does all the major digging and building and we mess around with a plastic spade, jumping in and out of the holes he's making, and at the end we look back and see the impressive thing he's built, in which we played a minor part, and we are glad.

Working together with God and together with others is what we were created to do, so there is no surprise that it is so exciting when we do it. It is at such points that we can see, at least a little, through the suffering.

How do you move beyond pain and suffering and horror? As I see it, the only way that things will make sense is if we limp forward together.

6

Short stories of hope

An important source of mental health support for children has been led by members of the Triborough Education Psychology Consultation. They, like me, have seen the centrality of hope in the aftermath of tragedy. Through parent and teacher workshops they have supported children and families and in some cases worked with the children directly.

Psychologist Jane Roller and her team have shared some of the stories of hope that have been fed back into their workshops, telling of positive things that have happened in the aftermath of the fire. They asked for stories of acts of kindness, courage, resilience and generosity that have given people comfort in the previous weeks. The following statements are anonymous and come from a variety of voices:

> A family resident in Grenfell Road just opened their front door and welcomed in an evacuated family to stay with them and made plans for their own children to stay with some friends so they had enough beds.

> Young men from the local community who were often considered 'bad boys', and had caused trouble in the past, rushed into the Tower to help people with little regard for their own safety and helped to save lots of people.

People who are Muslims broke their Ramadan fast to eat with the community in Iftar meals during the first few days as volunteers in centres. I feel that has brought the community together, that we know whom we can rely on and people who were never friends now feel a connection and a bond regardless of country of origin or faith.

Children were prepared to give up their toys and possessions to children who had lost theirs.

A Catholic cardinal from London came to visit children at one school, and sat with every class answering their questions with regard to death, heaven, religion and so on. He sat with them on the floor and was really down to earth and able to joke and laugh with the children.

David Walliams visited one local school and sat with each class to read stories and provide light relief and entertainment for the pupils, which was very well received.

Every pupil from a school in Walthamstow sent a card to a pupil at one of the affected primary schools to say they were thinking of them.

A local school took extraordinary initiative very quickly and supported every family affected by the fire by providing considerable financial assistance via raised funds within hours and days of the tragedy: they did not wait for the local authority response. The local community felt extremely well supported by their local school.

One primary school invited all their ex-Year 6 pupils (currently Year 7) to come back to meet with and talk to their previous teachers.

One secondary school in a neighbouring borough opened its doors to students from the school next to the Tower, Kensington Aldridge Academy (KAA). The Year 11 students went out of their way to make the KAA students feel welcome, with posters and by greeting students warmly around the school premises.

Following a parents' workshop, we heard about residents of a tower block meeting together to take action to increase their safety in the event of a fire, including purchasing public address speakers for each landing, setting up a text-messaging group for alerting neighbours, and working out plans for who would knock on whose door.

The local community were amazed to see several young people – who were known to the Youth Offending team and often getting in trouble – actively helping out in the community in the days following Grenfell. One young person was seen to donate from his own wallet to a family in need.

During Ramadan, Muslims believe that the doors to hell are closed and the doors to paradise are open.

One school participating in 'Green for Grenfell' said, 'It was amazing to see how the whole school community came together to support those affected and to donate funds. We raised the most amount of money we have raised as a school and had the best response we have received from families for a charity event.'

All the staff from one of the secondary schools closest to Grenfell came to the Grenfell area next day when the school was closed and helped to run rescue centres, sorting clothes and spending time with their pupils. They managed to get the school up and running again in three days, on a new site and in a (considerably smaller) primary school building. One of the teachers raised a phenomenal amount through setting up an online fundraising site.

One headteacher commented that children came into school bringing their pocket money to put into collection buckets.

A member of staff from Virgin Active was present on the first day, going around with the club's gym towels so that people who were evacuated could clean themselves down. She said, 'The feeling of everyone trying to help among all of the slow-motion chaos was so reassuring,' and felt that a lot of good came from the community coming together and supporting one another.

You can't really think everything will go well in life because bad things happen but you can expect help because that's what's happened after the fire. Everybody's been so supportive. No one thinks it didn't matter that much. Our school got a letter from a school in Cornwall asking if we are OK. I'm glad they care. If something happened to them I would care. I'm glad that I'm alive. It could've spread anywhere but it didn't.

(Jemie Doherty, aged ten)

Boxing

Within a few days of the fire some professionally printed posters were spread around, advertising a boxing event for kids who had been affected by the fire. I took my son and his friend to White City to participate. The temperature was 34 degrees and yet the kids were really keen to meet the boxers and learn to punch – and there was free food and drink! My son appreciated it because it was a welcome distraction organized at such short notice, only a week after the fire. The Dale Boxing Club was one of the venues destroyed by the fire so it was appropriate that boxing was one of the amazing opportunities offered to children in the wake of the fire. There were very special guests too, famous young boxers, role models for the boys to look up to.

General gratitude

I've grown up in this area and I always felt relatively safe but there have been times and certain streets that you wouldn't walk down because you feel unsafe, but I feel like that general vibe changed. People were making eye contact with each other more. Little things like when I get off a bus I always say, 'Thank you, driver!' but I've noticed more people doing that and people just being generally kinder to each other.   (Andreia, local resident)

Holiday clubs

The Council has always run a series of holiday clubs and play schemes. In the year following the Grenfell fire many of these were completely free for local residents, allowing children somewhere safe and constructive to go, and giving parents the chance to work or take a break without putting an added strain on their budget.

There was a phenomenal amount of other activities to do during the holidays. Every weekend there were fetes and festivals, all organized at extremely short notice. There was even a pop-up farm that appeared for a few hours. These things were great distractions for both children and parents and meant that those on a limited budget were able to enjoy days out very close to home. Most events were free unless they were fundraisers for Grenfell.

Cold water on a hot day

A small but simple act of kindness that touched my heart happened on Treadgold Street right in the area around the foot of the Tower. A person had recognized the needs of the community in the extreme heat and had left a jug of water with a linen cloth over the top and a pile of plastic cups. There was a sign saying, 'Please help yourself'. This gesture, so small in one way, was so significant. We may have nothing that we can share that is important to relief efforts, but for those walking in this emotion-ridden place a cup of water offered is a kindness worthy of Jesus himself. As he said: 'if anyone gives even a cup of cold water to one of these little ones who is my disciple, truly I tell you, that person will certainly not lose their reward' (Matthew 10.42).

Celebs felt it too

The list of celebrities who came to pay respects and even tried to help in some way was staggering – from grime artist Stormzy, who sang on the charity record (see the section below) and called the Government to account at his Glastonbury Festival set, to boxers, actors, singers, politicians. The Archbishop of Canterbury, the Prime Minister and even the Queen and Prince William came to share support.

Adele, the singer, was obviously affected. I believe she has a home fairly locally. She was reported singing to firefighters in their fire station, she went to the memorial service for children of a local school, and she also came and sang to a local play-centre during the summer holidays. Many of the children had no idea she was famous, but those who did were excited and pleased. Newspapers also report that she treated survivor children to a private screening of *Despicable Me 3* during the summer holidays, and she attended the service at St Paul's Cathedral.

U2, the biggest rock band in the world, gave a private concert solely for firefighters who had been involved in Grenfell. What an amazing gesture for those who were at the front line!

Songs for survivors

Many recent disasters have warranted their own charity single and Grenfell was no different. Simon Cowell of *X Factor* fame lives close to the area and admitted, 'I am watching the footage of the Grenfell Tower fire in London. Heartbreaking . . . We hope to confirm a record tomorrow which will raise some money for the many people affected by this tragedy. Making calls tonight.'

Speaking to *Good Morning Britain* by phone on Friday morning, Simon said:

I was watching the news and then I drove up to see the building which is only round the corner from me.

I've seen a lot of bad things, and there, you know, not far away from where I was sitting, I just . . . it really dawned on you. Honestly, it sent chills through me.

Seeing the building, it made a big impact. I think the thing that really hit home to me was when I was seeing that wall and I saw those messages and then when I saw how the residents immediately turned up with water and clothes and offers of shelter and everything else . . . that's when I thought, *I'm not just going to sit here and do nothing.*

For me, in my position, not to do something would be appalling. So I wrote to all the record label heads and I basically said, 'Let's all work together. There's a bigger cause here.'

The single, 'Bridge over Troubled Waters', a cover of the Simon and Garfunkel song, was the fastest-selling single this decade. This was a way people all over the world could donate money and keep Grenfell on their playlists. Every time the song is played you can remember those who suffered and died.

Another artist who wrote a more political tribute was hip-hop artist Lowkey, who wrote 'Ghosts of Grenfell', a moving song and video challenging the Council with questions and requesting justice. He lives opposite the Tower and was part of the community that was on the ground that night. He says, 'None of us have been the same . . . For me it's important that the music changes the lived tangible reality.'

Football hope

My son Joey and his friends are football mad. They love the competition, the running around and the chance to be with other like-minded children. The Westway sports centre has always run fantastic, reasonably priced sports camps through-out the summer holidays. After Grenfell they surpassed them-selves, providing free football coaching for nearly every single day of the summer holidays. What was even better this time was that both Chelsea Football Club and Queens Park Rangers (QPR) got involved, sending a ready supply of young and enthusiastic coaches. The boys were trained by people who played for local Premier and Championship teams.

These kinds of opportunities normally only arise for those who are committed to football and excel at it, not just those who like to have a weekly kick-around. This was a very special time for all the children who took part and also for the parents as it eased the burden of childcare over the holidays. When children have a lot of physical energy and you couple that with a lack of parental emotional energy, the combination can make for a disastrous summer! Sending Joey and his friends off to play football all day, and seeing him coming home exhausted and happy, made my summer much easier as I would have found it hard to cope, and I know other parents would have felt the same.

On a larger scale the football teams have also been keen to help out. On Saturday, 2 September there was a charity match, #Game4Grenfell, to lift the spirits of local residents and raise money for the Grenfell funds. Loftus Road, home of QPR, hosted the match. It was the idea of Sir Les Ferdinand, ex-Premier League footballer and current Queens Park Rangers Football Director. He said this of #Game4Grenfell: 'I spoke to some of the survivors and they were really pleased with the idea that we were doing this. They feel it will be great for some of the young kids and part of the healing process.' Les grew up on Hurstway Walk, one of the finger blocks below Grenfell Tower, and his rise to fame comes from humble roots. He has been trying to encourage healing and support victims in any way he can. He organized a host of celebrities, not limited to football players but including Marcus Mumford, Olly Murs, Sir Mo Farah, four firemen and also four survivors from Grenfell, to play in the match, which included a minute's silence at the start.

Selena Price Bennari, a local mum and lifelong resident who also grew up on Hurstway Walk, attended the match and said:

> It was quite emotional for me because I saw people I grew up with whom I hadn't seen for a few years. The most emotional moment, though, was when the survivors came on to play. It brought tears to my eyes and my children. I recognized Les Ferdinand from the estate, as my sister knew him. He felt the pain more because he grew up there.

Andy Evans, chief executive officer of Queens Park Rangers Trust, said, 'There are no real positives to take out of what happened at Grenfell Tower, but I think everybody across the world was taken aback by the community spirit that was shown.' QPR continues to try to help schools in the local area:

> In addition to the funds raised by the match, through their Premier League Primary Stars programme, QPR in the Community Trust is planning to provide pupils at primary schools in the area one-to-one support.

This includes their 'football as therapy' programme, drop-in football sessions and community festivals, as well as using partners to deliver training for teachers around mental health and dealing with grief/trauma.

(Premier League website, 31 August 2017)

This is a much-needed service and hopefully will reach some children who need it. As for the match, 'Today was about making sure people remembered,' said QPR chairman Tony Fernandes. 'It was about making sure no one ever forgets what happened.'

This is a crucial lesson for the UK, and part of the Grenfell legacy will be continually trying to ensure that such a tragedy never happens again.

Cat with nine lives?

Grenfell Tower, like other homes in the region, also hosted pets. One lady, Kerry O'Hara, was devastated when escaping from her sixth-floor flat that she had to leave her cat Rosey behind.

'When I looked down the hallway before I turned to go out the door, I could see she was sitting on the sofa. And I had to leave her because I couldn't bring her out.' Kerry had hoped to put her in her cat basket and bring her, but she didn't have time. Kerry never expected to see Rosey again, assuming that the worst had happened and Rosey was another victim of the fire. Kerry attends Latymer Community Church, and prayers were said for her and her cat.

However, the story doesn't end there. Kerry says:

Two months later I discovered that Rosey managed to get out by herself. She kept returning to Grenfell Tower, looking for me and probably looking for food. Then eventually she was caught by a lady in her garden and she was handed to a vet. They rang me and said, 'We've got your cat Rosey!' and that was after two months of her being on the street. She is four years old. I've had her since she was a little ball of fluff, a kitten, and she's never been out – she's an indoor cat. When I heard that she was alive I was a bit hysterical and I had lots of questions: 'Is she burnt?' 'Is she OK?' And they told me that she was OK – she didn't have any marks except a scratch on her nose. Apart from that and a bit of weight loss, she was OK. It was a bit overwhelming. I didn't think I was ever going to see her again. She got out, and no one will ever know how it happened, but she did.

Holidays for locals

A lovely neighbour of mine, Naima, her husband, and sons Yonis and Yusuf live in a tower facing Grenfell. They were invited to go on an expenses-paid holiday to give them some space and rest away from west London, organized by a Somalian community group. Her sons were at school with children who died and they told me there were 'no words' to describe how they felt about this. However, when I asked about their holiday they became animated and told me the whole story. Yonis, aged ten, said:

> We took a coach to Southampton and then we took the ferry to the Isle of Wight and then a coach to the PGL [an adventure holiday centre] and Mum came with us. When we arrived they gave us keys to our own bungalow. Every morning they would come and wake us up at eight o'clock for breakfast. The food was a very nice buffet. We played football. We did climbing and archery. The best thing was we had a water fight. It was too cold to swim in the sea.

Naima added:

> We were there five days and we had a lovely time. It was organized by the Somalian community organization but there were also Eritrean families too, many of whom lived in Grenfell. There were two buses full of people who went. They were all from the local area.

She told me all about the bereaved families who were there, but also about the various activities and fun, and how they danced in the evenings. She had a fantastic time. The community feeling was very strong and they enjoyed themselves, but at the end they still had to come home to 'that'. (At this point Naima gestured to the Tower, visible from their living room window.)

Cornwall Hugs Grenfell

Cornwall Hugs Grenfell is a charity that was started to give people from the Tower and surrounding area, and firefighters and their families, a holiday in Cornwall. Its members were trying to organize a second group holiday to Cornwall but couldn't find accommodation for the people who might be interested. Esmé, the organizer, texted a group of Christians who were praying for the project and asked them to pray for accommodation. Within an hour a man called and asked if he could help. He was a resort manager and so Esmé asked for 12 units. He phoned back in the afternoon and it was all agreed.

Megabus donated a coach and driver for a whole week.

Thus the holiday went ahead and was a success. Things the holidaymakers learned in Cornwall were brought home. Esmé says, 'People told me they were going to do more walking when they went back to London. Someone told me he was going to take up kayaking because there is a canal near home.' They also became a group of friends who supported each other in London.

Esmé has received some feedback from the Londoners who visited Cornwall. One young person said:

We went to the beach and it was really, really nice, especially when we got to do the surfing. 'Cos in London we really don't have that opportunity so having it here is really good. I felt really happy and everything, 'cos I kept dropping and I got back up and tried again.

Another resident commented about Cornwall:

> It gives you like a fresh air. Coming here takes off like all
> the bad memories that happened in London and when
> you come here in the sun and going to the beach it takes
> all that memory off and starts anew. It's been good for my
> family 'cos we got to do something we all enjoy.

A girl aged 12 was a guest on the Falmouth Group Holiday
(her family lived in one of the blocks that were evacuated on
the night of the fire and that family of seven has been living in
a hotel ever since). She told me:

> I just wanted to say thank you and blessings to Cornwall,
> to everybody who put this together – the hearts, the souls,
> the strength, the courage that went into bringing us down
> from London, not knowing us, just feeling for us and
> feeling everything that we felt. I think the world should do
> more of this. This is what humanity is about and Cornwall
> is a great example of humanity. Thank you!

A mother of four on the Falmouth Group Holiday said:

> It's meant a lot. I've felt a transformation in myself. I've
> felt myself unwind immediately we got here, which was
> really strange. The knots in my shoulders, the rocks on my
> shoulders, dissipated. I've seen my daughter transform
> from feeling weepy all the time into someone who feels
> and looks elevated. I've seen my baby granddaughter,

who's only 17 weeks old, enjoying the holiday and wanting
to participate in everything, even though that might sound
strange. I've seen my other two grandchildren literally free
up themselves, their minds, their bodies, and just enjoy.
It's good to be around the people who came on this
holiday, especially the [Grenfell] locals.

The highlight was the music therapy. It heightened my
spirituality. I connected spiritually; I got messages
spiritually. I was relaxed; I was chilled out. The
atmosphere in that room was magical.

What would she take back from Cornwall, returning to the
environment around the Tower?

Going back to Kensington, I feel I've discovered a form of
balance, that there's more to life than the tragedy we've
all had to endure, and I know we're going back into that
environment, but at least we can look back and cherish these
memories in order to move forward. These are memories I
will draw on. Cornwall is a place I will never forget. The
emotions that are coming out in me, now it's time to leave,
are very positive. My tears now are positive tears. When I
came, my tears were very negative and hurtful tears.

As the week ended, parents spoke enthusiastically about the
holiday, citing unbroken sleep, laughter, family connection
around the dining table, and 'a suitcase full of new memories'
as key benefits.

'Our kids are much happier. They are sleeping better, and all the questions about the Tower have stopped,' said one mum. 'They are also more confident to leave my side, which has been difficult since the fire.'

'It means the world to us to see our children smiling and laughing from their hearts again,' said a mother of four, who continued:

> I lost a close friend and my son's best friend in the fire. We have had emotional support from different professionals, but coming to Cornwall was indescribable therapy, just by talking to the kind and welcoming people and being in the fresh air.

One of the pieces of feedback from a local headteacher was that after the holiday the children were more confident; they had more self-esteem, more focus and were more settled.

One guest chose a particular day of his holiday just to cook and cook and cook and cook. He left Esmé Page, the holiday organizer, with a washing-up bowl full of marinated chicken ready to cook. He returned to London thinking about how he could become a chef. The holiday gave him distance and perspective, and confidence to think about doing something different.

Grenfell survivors were not the only ones who received good things from the holiday – their Cornish hosts also benefited. 'We felt privileged to meet such remarkable people,' said Sandy

Richards, family services coordinator at Penhaligon's Friends, a child bereavement charity in Cornwall that supported the trip. 'They've taught us the meaning of a community. The strength and friendships that have grown between parents during the crisis are evident.'

World in motion

Jackie Blanchflower, a local resident, remembers:

I loved the human chain we had here, moving donated goods from upstairs [at Latymer Community Church] to under the Westway, through to [the offices of] John Brown Media. It was like the world gathered side by side as a human chain, passing out the donations. There was a feeling that we are one humanity and when we hurt we all hurt the same. That was really powerful. You could identify people from a Muslim background, a Sikh background, a Christian background and those from no faith at all, all working together as one. There were probably more than 100 people involved. It took about 30 people to get the stuff out of the doors of the church, and [the John Brown offices are] quite a long way from there.

You just had to go outside and shout 'Volunteers!' and people would come in and just do what was needed. There was real selfless giving. We had a week when we didn't need money – we could just ring up businesses and they would just give it to us.

Grenfell Tower, 2.12 a.m., 14 June 2017

Grenfell Tower, 2.55 a.m., 14 June 2017,
showing rapid spread of fire

People standing silently to look at the Tower

Volunteers working to sort out a small proportion of the donations

We had to ask visitors for respect and gentleness

People shared their hearts

Justice and openness were high on people's agenda

Boxing event organized a week after the fire

Artwork sent from all over the world in solidarity

Guerrilla gardening in action

The initial #24hearts project

24hearts poster

Kids on the Green indoors, learning new skills

Christmas for Grenfell party poster

Graffiti making political statements

Graffiti with a spiritual element

The Tower after the fire

We saw God answer specific prayers for individuals. The wider Church came in and helped. The Anglican church helped us: even though we're not an Anglican church, they provided people to help on our rota. A friend came in and ran a kitchen for two weeks. This is how the body of the Church came together. So many people have given so much. We saw the reality of human nature, the good and the bad.

There was also a service, held in the open air outside Latymer Community Church on the first Sunday, that spilled on to the road. 'The service was awesome because it gave people opportunities to come together,' said Jackie. She recalls:

The sung worship had the biggest impact on people because it recognized that God is still God, even in the midst of the devastation and the brokenness, and that God was still in control even when nobody at all was. There was real unity in our grief and sorrow and we appreciated the care of those who came and put on the service. It was a really powerful moment when the fire engine came past and also when the firemen came down to the memory wall. They had been getting some criticism, but they gave so much.

A fire engine drove slowly through the crowds of worshippers and, as it did, the firefighters received a massive ovation of claps and cheers – thanks for all they did and were continuing to do.

Jackie also told me about a donated guitar. A person came into Latymer Community Church offering a really great guitar because he realized how distraught he would be if he lost an instrument in such a terrible way. Someone had just had a conversation with a parent whose child had lost her guitar and was able to connect the two together.

Unite for Grenfell

Many people hosted events, either as fundraisers or to bolster local people. One of these was called Unite for Grenfell and took place on 15 July 2017, organized by local resident Montrise Eastmond-Lewis, who is deeply involved in the Notting Hill Carnival, together with some of her friends. Here she gives her account of the event and how it came about:

> It was a mixture of live performances from local artists, children's activities such as face painting and a bouncy castle, and we also got a few caterers to provide food and donate the proceeds to the cause.
>
> The day of the fire I went down to the Tower, which was still alight, and the devastation really hit me. The Grenfell Tower was a part of my childhood. I had friends who lived there. I went down to the Rugby Portobello with donations from myself and clients from my workplace. It was overwhelming how much support they had received, but the confusion of *What now?* really hit me.

I couldn't sleep that night. My eight-year-old son was scared to sleep because we live high up as well. I was overcome with emotion – and the idea just came to me.

I have always been a big part of Notting Hill Carnival and very involved in community events, such as playing steel pan in the park. I put the idea on social media . . . [I wanted to host] something that celebrated the diverse cultures because that is literally my favourite part of living in Ladbroke Grove. We wanted something that brought us together – hence 'Unite' – and gave people something to look forward to.

I knew I wanted to do a fundraiser that actually got the community involved. I wanted to do something that I knew wouldn't benefit a big corporation but would bring the community together and make sure the proceeds went to where they were actually needed.

When I first put it on social media I was expecting my usual friends to say 'Yeah, sounds good!' and get involved. But the actual response was *amazing*! You could literally see how much the community did care and did want to come together. I had so many artists come forward to say they wanted to perform, and so many carnival bands say they wanted to do their part. It was beautiful to see.

I saw hope in the community spirit. We all wanted to work together. We all wanted to help. We all wanted to make sure the lives lost were never forgotten . . . We had been failed but we stuck together. We did more together than the

Government if you ask me. Not just my event but the mosque, the Tabernacle [a creative arts and community centre], the churches and so on. We realized these people needed us, so we tried to give them as much help as we could.

Bags of joy

The Body Shop provided 100 Bags for Life, filled with toiletries to be shared with survivors, evacuees and those who had suffered. I was blessed to be able to give out some of these bags, and people were so happy to receive them. They helped people to feel loved and valued.

Random kindness and gifts

As just one family that lives in the area, we were showered with affection and prayer by our friends. Several people sent us money to go for days out and trips to the cinema. My own secret coping mechanism was collecting toy trading cards from the supermarket and putting them into albums for my children. I was given enough cards to fill four albums, and I never spent a penny on any of them because they were all donated to me, including the albums! The range of the gifts was enormous, even including help with housework for a few weeks when I was struggling to keep up with the normal tasks of life.

Bramley Road, the main road that Latimer tube station is on – a road that was shut by police when the fire was at its height – became a hub of activity day and night for several weeks and still has a memory wall and tributes along it. One night I heard a lot of noise at about midnight and went out, only to discover a small band of children armed with instruments playing a trumpet tribute to the Tower. There were also rappers who stood on the street and performed, together with other musicians, all trying to convey their emotions. There was always free food out for people to share, for anyone who wanted it, not just locals or survivors. So many people came to pay their respects from all over the UK, and I made new friends. One lady I was speaking to was suddenly interrupted by someone asking for an autograph; it turned out she was an actress from *Bad Girls* who had been recognized.

Art therapy

Therapy for children has been key for local parents. There has been a proliferation of people willing and able to help. Local mum and art therapist Susan Rudnik set up a huge art therapy project in a local community centre. The project was so successful that it will now run permanently. This has been an amazing source of support for troubled kids and is definitely part of the inheritance of the fire that will leave a permanent mark of improvement in the area.

Business bonus

Many large companies and businesses have also helped out and given generously. Bramley's, the local indoor adventure playground, offered free play and a meal for those most affected.

A team from TalkTalk, the broadband provider, which operates locally, sent local residents this email:

Hello. Working close by, we know how distressing the past weeks have been for everyone in our local community. We also know access to your home has been impacted by the police restrictions put in place. As a team we wanted to make a small gesture, and to give you one less thing to worry about. We will cover your broadband monthly package charges for the next three months, so you won't have to pay anything for the time that you're out of your home. You don't need to do anything – we'll do this automatically for you and it will appear as credits on your July–September broadband bills.

We're actively supporting all our customers who lived in Grenfell Tower and the local efforts to raise funds for those needing support. We will also continue to monitor the information from the authorities and help where we can. If you do have questions or need support please contact our executive team who will personally look after you. Our thoughts are with everyone at this difficult time.

The manager who emailed this had personally volunteered as part of the relief effort. He and his colleagues had seen what was going on and wanted to help. The big companies were full of people who felt our pain. They wanted to be part of helping suffering people too.

Christmas party

Local resident Stevan Racz organized a 'Christmas Party for Grenfell'. He said:

I watched a documentary which showed actual video footage from someone's phone on it. In the footage you could hear the screams of the people in the flats. It has haunted me since I watched it. When I was approached to help a certain group achieve its Christmas plans, I asked if we could extend help to those who lived surrounding the Tower, who would have witnessed the horrors and heard those screams. I had volunteered for Grenfell before, so I knew volunteers who would benefit the campaign. I contacted them and each one joined without hesitation. We all had the same agenda, helping those who have had it hard after Grenfell. It's not much, but if we raised spirits and put smiles on faces it was all worth it.

He described what happened:

In total we raised £24,000. It was raised in 25 days. We had a core team of 16 volunteers and about an additional 20 or more helpers for things like wrapping etc. The event, I suspect, had in excess of 600 people. We worked that out from the number of Santa presents handed out and the food that was eaten.

The campaign was split into three projects. The first project was to give survivors and the displaced/bereaved a special gift of their choosing – roughly 300 affected in total. We have handed out a fair amount of these and are actively pushing to reach the rest. The second project was the event. The third project is dealing with the leftovers. It's called the 'legacy campaign' where we aim to use leftover money and gifts to give to the local schools, nurseries and youth centres. We will buy them equipment of their choosing that children can get continued use out of.

I took my kids to the party. It was phenomenal. There was a realistic Santa, an elf who was the same height as my children, a host of fabulous entertainers, popcorn and candy floss on tap, real reindeer to visit, virtual-reality headsets, party games, endless gifts, snacks and drinks – and all free. Many people in the local community came out and had an amazing time. It was a child's paradise. Several months on from the fire, it meant a lot for the community to come together like this and to know that there were still people caring for us and thinking of us.

March of peace

Every month on the 14th there is a silent march to remember Grenfell. Locals want to keep remembering those who were lost, and peacefully keep justice for Grenfell on the agenda. This is a powerful sign to remind the world that we are still here. Grenfell must never be forgotten, because as soon as we forget the lessons we learned we will be opening a door for a similar tragedy to happen in the future. The marches will continue until everyone has a home and justice is done through the investigations.

This has been just a small picture of the massive outpourings of generosity that surrounded the area.

7

Where the streets have no name

Inhabitants of North Kensington are extremely proud to live here and many will tell you it's the best place to live in London. There is every advantage for residents to enjoy. Being a royal borough, Kensington Palace is not far from us, and the whole of Hyde Park is laid out for our enjoyment. We also have the gorgeous Holland Park, a place so green and spacious that you can almost forget you're in central London. One thing the Council does exceptionally well is managing parks. There are parks and playgrounds all over the borough and most in good repair. Children are well catered for.

Jimmy Bracher has lived in Kensington his whole life. He offers his perspective:

> I feel lucky to have grown up in this area because it gives you a good outlook and a good wide-ranging view of life because it's such a mixed bag in every way. In terms of the architecture, in terms of the ethnicity, in terms of, for want of a better word, class. You've got everything here and I think it is a great area for kids to grow up in. The problem is that the balance is changing, and more and more I think, *Do I really want my kids to grow up here? And will they be able to? Will they have the same problems*

we have but worse? In Notting Hill the houses are very nice and big, so people with money started moving in. They used to be slums, then they were split into flats, and then they were brought back into houses again.

There is always major refurbishment going on in the large, gracious garden-square streets. Homeowners are keen to sink basements to allow for more space, although the Council is now opposing this practice more regularly.

Jimmy comments:

There are advantages to gentrification. The streets are safer and cleaner. There are nice places to go. I'm not someone who harks back to the days when there'd be fights in the pubs every night. It's just that the balance is wrong and the local working-class people are under siege and have been for the last 35 years.

In North Kensington we also have the Portobello Road, which still retains its magic for me, no matter how many times I trip over tourists on my way into a discount shop or nearly kill pedestrians who think the street is car-free all week. 'Sorry, only on Saturdays!' It's a great place just to wander around and breathe in the atmosphere.

Notting Hill is full of private squares and gardens surrounded by beautiful homes, and some of them include housing association and council properties. We also have many landmarks from the film *Notting Hill*: the famous blue door, bookshop and garden square that appear in that film. Even Richard Curtis's own home is a feature every year during Comic Relief as he decorates his house with an abundance of red noses.

Ladbroke Grove runs like a ski run through the area, skirting the edges of rich and poor areas. Jimmy comments on how the place has changed:

> A lot of the roads were longer in the past. The growth of gentrification was exponential. There have always been wealthy people in the area but they didn't start moving into the rougher parts until the late 1980s and early 1990s. In the last ten years it's been unstoppable. The pubs started closing. All my family moved out. The estates are the last little pockets of people I call 'locals'.

The Notting Hill race riots in 1958 happened just metres from Grenfell Tower. They were allegedly sparked by a married couple having an argument outside Latimer Road tube station. The husband was black and the wife white. Some Teddy Boys subsequently attacked the houses of West Indian (as they were referred to then, latterly Caribbean) families on Bramley Road.

After this, to bring people together and to celebrate Caribbean culture, the Carnival was started. In modern times during the August Bank Holiday over a million revellers crowd the local streets to enjoy the Notting Hill Carnival. Residents are divided about Carnival. Some love it and spend their entire year preparing for it, while others leave before the festivities begin and return only after the streets are clean and quiet again. Carnival is loud, proud and irrepressible, and its roots are intertwined with the local culture and the connections between people of different ethnicities mixing together. What began as a celebration of Caribbean people and their culture and expression has become one that everyone is welcome to enjoy.

North Kensington is very much an area to itself. My sister once decided to visit the museums in South Kensington, travelling from our previous home in Cricklewood. She mistakenly took a bus that landed her in North Kensington, so she set off to walk to the museums. *How far can it be?* she thought. After she had walked for half an hour and still hadn't reached her destination, she realized that it was a long way!

'North Ken' and 'South Ken' are sharply divided. There are beautiful houses belonging to the rich and famous just a few moments' walk from the whole area surrounding Grenfell. South Ken is the tourist area of extreme wealth and privilege. North Ken was always the Labour red-voting area at the top of a Conservative blue-voting borough! Most of the social housing of the borough is in this part and it is colourful, fun, sometimes dangerous, but always moving and changing.

This area is broadly called Notting Hill. Back in the 1960s, residents were practically giving away some of the homes here, as Notting Hill had slum areas. The council ward it sits in is Notting Dale, formerly Notting Barns. People refer to it as Latimer Road or Ladbroke Grove, and even more recently, people call the area Grenfell. When filling in forms that require a second and third line of address, I usually just put 'London' for both!

Jimmy remembers his childhood:

The area was much more working class, quite dangerous, but with a lot of community spirit. Ladbroke Grove was pretty much slums all the way down to Notting Hill Gate. There were loads of pubs, three or four on every street. The estates were quite rough. When I was a kid I wasn't allowed to go in them but as you're a kid you do anyway. I used to walk home from Latimer Road past Grenfell in my school uniform and I'd quite often get robbed, perhaps two or three times a month. First question would always be, 'What school do you go to?' If you heard that question you knew you were about to be mugged. Older kids would push you about and take your change. You made sure you never had your personal stereo visible! My 'get out of jail' card was my older cousins, who used to be quite notorious around here, and when I mentioned their names muggers would give me my stuff back and tell me I could go. I told my cousins about this. They're all settled now and they find it really funny.

The white working-class families who lived here in the 1950s mostly did not have adequate housing or facilities, although Harrow School and Rugby School set up the Harrow Club (a youth club) and the Rugby Portobello Club (a facility that embraces youth and family support work).

This was an area also where West Indian families had arrived and settled ever since the 1948 *Empire Windrush* era. When we first moved on to the Silchester West estate, my white neighbour was surprised that another white English family was moving in because she had only ever seen the white English families moving out. Allegedly, some of the rioters in 1958 came from my own square!

The area is now exceptionally diverse. The main faith-groups are Muslim, Christian, Sikh and Jewish, as we have mosques, churches, a gurdwara and a synagogue, all just off the main road running through. Even that main road through the area is unsure of its identity, starting as St Helens Gardens, turning into Bramley Road, then curving round into St Ann's Villas and ending at Royal Crescent. The Latimer Road after which the tube is named is nowhere to be seen – it's about 500 metres away.

The community is diverse. My neighbours are Turkish, Pakistani, Irish, English, Welsh, Scottish, Portuguese, Brazilian, Spanish, French, Jordanian, Eritrean, Iraqi, Caribbean from many different islands, Moroccan, Ghanaian and Somalian. Most nationalities have their own communities where people meet together with others from the same background (although many were born in the UK). However, like a Venn diagram, all the communities connect with each other. Eritreans, for example, are either Muslim or Christian. The Christians worship either in their Eritrean Orthodox church or another local church. But families connect easily across this divide.

Jimmy observes:

When I was younger there were lots of North Africans, and since the 1950s there's always been the West Indian element. Then there are the Irish – I always forget to mention them because I'm one of them! In the 1980s, more North Africans started arriving. As the English and Irish working class moved out, other ethnic mixes took their places.

The sports centre below the Grenfell Tower has become the central hub for all nations. There is space for the children to play, and a café. Swimming lessons and sports lessons are reasonably priced, so everyone meets there. Despite our differences the community is strong.

But what about the wider borough? Kensington and Chelsea Council is the smallest borough in London but one of the most densely populated. It is in fact the second smallest borough in the whole of the UK.

Kensington and Chelsea's motto is adapted from the opening words of the Latin version of Psalm 133: *Quam bonum in unum habitare.* It means 'How good it is to dwell in unity'. This seems slightly ironic considering the massive divide there has always been between North and South. North Kensington has always been happy to coexist with South Kensington, provided it is able to continue with its market, carnival and colourful diversity. The problems come when people no longer feel welcome or included in the place they have called home for so long.

A biblical welcome is one where we invite the strangers and aliens into our homes and towns. Kensington does offer a welcome to all. The Council's website says:

> Some 179,000 people live in the borough, but thousands more come here each day to work or visit and around 30,000 visitors stay each night. There is an extraordinary ethnic and cultural diversity; nearly half of the residents were born outside the UK, coming from 90 countries and speaking over 100 different languages. It is the smallest borough in London but has the highest residential density. Although known as one of the wealthiest areas in the country a few wards are still considered to be within the ten per cent most deprived wards in England.

This open welcome, however, clearly does not necessarily include giving people adequate living arrangements!

Jimmy is someone who has always lived in some form of social housing, and his experience is that the housing stock is not well maintained. 'If you need something done you have to do it yourself,' he says. 'The Council won't do it because they don't have the funding.' It is interesting that such a rich borough does not find the resources to look after its more vulnerable residents, a pattern that was obvious from the cladding of Grenfell. The outside looked good but inside it was rotten, and residents had repeatedly raised concerns about inadequate fire safety measures. Jimmy claims:

> It's no surprise to me that Grenfell Tower wasn't safe because of cost-cutting. It's no surprise to anyone who has

lived in council housing because everyone has the same experience. You take it for granted that [if you have concerns or need repairs] nothing is going to be done. The fire shone a light on the Council. Everyone can see it for what it is. Kensington and Chelsea shows the stark contrast in the way the Council has run things. They spent tens of millions paving over Exhibition Road [in South Kensington, where the museums are] but can't spend money covering over gas pipes to keep families safe. I hope the attention Grenfell has brought to the plight of poorer people in the area won't diminish.

Jimmy describes his experience of the fire:

When I first saw it I was distraught for the people in there. You could see how bad it was straight away. It was like part of your soul burning. I grew up in the shadow of Grenfell Tower and it was symbolic for people of my generation. Grenfell stuck out because it was bigger than the other four towers. Over the years I've visited friends and family who lived there, or used it as a cut-through. I've always hung around the building because as kids that was just where we used to hang out.

My second reaction was, *This is going to be the excuse they need to get rid of everyone.* Ironically for now, it's had the opposite effect, but I'm a bit cynical about what happens next. I think the whole estate will be gone in 12–15 years. When you feel under siege and the community has dwindled, and you see Grenfell Tower burning, it just feels like another part of the area's soul is going to get ripped out.

I knew there was a strong community spirit in the area, but even I was surprised how well people reacted. Everyone chipped in. Everyone realized what they had in common.

Normally you are aware of how you're different. Then Grenfell happened and we realized one thing we've got in common is that we're skint, and we should stick together.

As Jimmy recognizes, the community bonded together for different reasons. Some made ties that would never be broken, while others established more casual friendships, but something of the Blitz spirit had been released and people were making new friends among their neighbours.

Montrise Eastmond-Lewis has lived in the area all her life. She commented:

The hope I see for the future would be safe social housing, and no more gentrification. We grew up around here and we shouldn't be pushed out. Your salary should not determine whether or not your home is safe and whether or not you have the right to stay in the same area where you grew up, your parents grew up and your grandparents grew up. I hope things will change. I hope now that my family will be looked at as equals so that if my children grow up and are not millionaires they can stay in the borough, as the fourth generation of my family to do so, and be able to live in a safe home.

This is a reasonable request that we could all echo for our own areas, but will it happen in Notting Hill?

Since the Grenfell fire, the community has been very busy. Many people are involved in some way or another with the after-effects of the fire, whether it be attending counselling or therapy, or encouraging others to seek help. There has been an explosion of creativity, from gardening projects, graffiti projects and poetry groups to art blossoming everywhere on the streets, and so many events are organized to keep the community spirit up, to raise funds or to commemorate those who died. North Kensington is fighting back against despair and proving why it is an incredible place to live. It is not a place with no name, but one with many names, full of beauty, diversity and creativity.

8

Hope unleashed

The biggest story of hope must be how the firefighters rescued so many. They saved around 65 people from the smoke-filled hell of the burning Tower, and our community will be eternally grateful. Those people would have died had they not been rescued. Sadly, some of them did not survive, despite the best efforts of the medical staff, but the firefighters did everything they could in the most unimaginable of conditions.

In each of these stories of hope there is an unspoken question: if God was helping some people to escape, why did so many die?

I truly don't know the answer. The courts will decide how to apportion blame for the spread of the fire, but my mission is to try to bring hope, to spread hope where the flames spread only disaster and destruction. God is present and active in the world where there is also an enemy, the devil, who seeks 'to steal and kill and destroy' (John 10.10). God sent Jesus to bring life in all its fullness, and this fullness allows us to move from desperation to hope.

Here is a story told by one firefighter:

I've been a firefighter since 2004 and I've always had an interest in the Fire Service due to family connections.

Seeing their real sense of job satisfaction and hearing stories of exciting incidents they attended inspired me. I guess you could say I never grew out of my childhood fascination with fire engines!

Latimer Road is not an area of London I know well. However, like everybody else on duty, firefighters and officers are a resource that can be used anywhere in London or even nationally, depending on shortfalls or demand.

It started as a normal night for us. The speed and the ferocity with which the fire took hold and spread seemed highly unusual. I have no interest in how the media work or why they sensationalize things, but without being insensitive or flippant it did look spectacular. I think the most accurate word is 'unprecedented'! There have been previous high-rise fires such as in Lakanal House where the fire jumped floors, but in this case all four sides were on fire, affecting almost the entire building. This is something even senior firefighters with many years on the job have never seen. Most sadly, the huge loss of life involved in this tragedy set this incident apart from the rest. It's still hard to think about how many people were trapped with no way of escaping and how we were unable to reach them. On the scene there were many conflicting reports on the numbers of people who may have lost their lives, or were unaccounted for.

With the various regulations surrounding high-rise buildings it's something that shouldn't happen. Fire safety is not my area of expertise, and investigations are obviously taking place, so it would be wrong of me to say whether a specific regulation was or wasn't broken. I don't have access to the information but do believe concerns had previously been raised about the cladding. In such a case it would then be the Council's responsibility to act.

The fact that there was no loss of life or serious physical injury to any members of the emergency services was a miracle in such circumstances. I guess what remains are the mental/emotional injuries. I have personally attended a couple of counselling sessions, and felt a sense of peace and support from the thoughts and prayers that surrounded me that night and moving forward.

There was real concern surrounding the safety of the building and the risks the fire services were taking. I was aware from messages of support that a lot of people were praying for everybody involved and that was a real encouragement. I must admit there were moments when I was scared and apprehensive. Knowing I was not alone gave me the confidence to carry on and keep my nerves in check. I believe prayers were answered in that I was kept safe, and was able to make quick and efficient decisions. I was aware that the job was bigger than any one person.

There were so many acts of courage and bravery that night. Under Fire Service policy, you are limited for safety reasons in the number of times you can wear a breathing apparatus. But people went on volunteering, in essence breaking the rules. Others were taking their breathing apparatus masks off to try to conserve air, and risking smoke inhalation on the way up. This is extremely dangerous, and I saw some very fit firefighters I know coming out of the building completely exhausted.

I was encouraged to see how colleagues and friends all pulled together with a common goal, far beyond the call of duty. There is often banter or mickey-taking between different crews, but that night people seemed more genuinely concerned about each other's welfare. This was particularly true of senior managers.

As firefighters, some of us may be guilty of portraying a 'rufty-tufty' image at times, so we are grateful for continued prayers for everyone's well-being. Our control room staff, who are the unseen side of the Fire Brigade (the heroes in headsets), had exceptional challenges. Some were in direct contact by phone with people trapped on the upper floors, and had to inform these families that we were trying our hardest but might not be able to reach them.

We hugely value the volunteers such as the Salvation Army and other relief teams, who were incredibly kind and encouraging. We so much appreciate the work they do, giving up their time to provide refreshments. It's a great example of service.

Local businesses also donated various resources and although I haven't been back, I know returning crews have received particular encouragement and kindness from the local community.

Fatima Alves was a resident of Grenfell Tower. She has been a Christian for many years, and as we spoke it was clear she had been through many struggles but always kept Jesus central in these trials. She and her family have been in the press regularly because they are courageous and have persevered through everything, maintaining a positive attitude in difficult times. Here is some of her story:

As a child my parents never had to force me to go to church. I was always very involved. Even when as an adult I had to work on Sundays, I still managed to slip out and go to church.

That night of the fire my cousin from South Africa and her daughter came for dinner. We all went to a Portuguese restaurant. Then Ines, my daughter, wanted to study for her exam so we all went home. We stayed in the sitting room talking until 20 minutes past midnight. My cousin saw the time and said, 'I must go and get a taxi,' but we offered to drop her back at her hotel. Ines was asleep already and my son Tiago was on his computer in his room, so my husband and I took her home.

When we came back everything was normal. We called the lift, but there were two men waiting in the lobby who had been drinking and we were keen to avoid sharing a lift with them. [When it came we stepped in.] I pushed the button for the thirteenth floor and the doors shut – but then they opened again and the men got in. They pressed for the fourth floor. When the doors opened on the fourth floor we saw smoke and decided to leave the lift. We thought, *Where there is smoke there is fire!*, and chose to climb the stairs instead.

At this point my husband realized he'd left his phone in the car.

'Can you go to the garage and get it while I fetch the children down?' he said. It was about 1 a.m. I went back downstairs and the firefighters arrived so I stayed at the door to let them in. When I asked them if it was safe to stay in the building they said, 'No, you stay here.'

'But my husband and children are in the flat!' I exclaimed. They asked me which floor and I told them the thirteenth. They instructed me to make my family stay inside the flat and to close the doors and windows.

I didn't have my phone because I had left it on charge at home, and my husband's phone was in the car. I buzzed him from the intercom at the front door, but when he picked up it wasn't working so I couldn't speak to him.

I then went to the garage to get his phone, and walked around the outside to see where the fire was. Meanwhile my husband came down with the children. He told me he'd woken all the neighbours: 'They'll be angry with me, but I don't care.' If you look at the list of those who died, there are none from the thirteenth floor, thanks to Miguel Alves.

On the thirteenth floor we were like a family. We would knock and ask for a bit of sugar or an onion. As they trooped downstairs I saw one man was missing. All the other neighbours were safe. My husband had knocked on his door but when he received no answer assumed that he was away. I kept ringing his phone, ringing, ringing, but he was in a very deep sleep and when he finally answered I told him not to panic but that there was a fire.

He was grumpy that someone was ringing and when he saw it was my husband's phone he wondered, *What does this guy want, phoning at this time?* When I explained about the fire he was badly scared, but I stayed on the phone speaking with him until he had left the building.

I saw fire at a window. Then the window exploded and the fire roared up and up and up, burning uncontrollably. The police arrived and they told us to go: 'Don't stay here as it might collapse!'

We went to Silchester Road for maybe 15 or 20 minutes and then on to our friends' house. We stayed in their house on the fourth floor, watching the Tower on fire. My friend's husband said, 'Come in from the balcony – don't stay out there!' But as I watched the fire burning my bedroom window and then my son's room and then my daughter's room and the kitchen window, I knelt down at that moment and started to pray. My son said, 'Mum, let's go to the bedroom and pray!' So my son, my friend and I went to her room and we prayed the Sorrowful Mysteries of the Rosary. We prayed to save as many people as possible, but especially the Portuguese family we knew that was still in there.

Later on my friends asked me, 'If you have given your life to Jesus, why have all these things happened to you?' It was a terrible time. Yet even as I sat on my friend's balcony watching the fire I remembered to say, 'God, I trust you and I love you and I know you have better things for us.'

My husband rang his friend on the twenty-first floor, a man who used to play football with him. He said, 'Listen, Marcio, there is a fire in the building. Get out!'

Marcio said, 'The firefighters told us to stay in. There's a lot of smoke in the hall.'

My husband said, 'Well, they know what they're doing.'

Later he rang again to see if Marcio and his family were out of the building, but they were still in the flat. My husband shouted at him, 'Marcio, you leave now! Otherwise you are going to die!'

'No, but the firefighters said to stay. We can't go out – the smoke is too thick.'

'If you stay, you're all going to die! Leave now!' my husband screamed at him.

I realized that was the end. We saw the flames on the twenty-first floor and they were still there. It was that moment we started praying to Our Lady to protect them. I prayed and begged God to save them.

We didn't want to ring again because we were frightened about what had happened. A little later I rang again, but no one answered. I thought that was a good sign – but of course the phone had been destroyed in the fire.

We watched everything all night. I didn't know it was on the news. I couldn't take my eyes off it.

I thank God we were in a safe place. Even though I saw my flat in flames, the most traumatic thing was seeing people at windows, begging for help. It was the most terrible thing.

Later that day someone called to tell us Marcio and his family had all died. I refused to accept it because I had prayed and begged God. Later still, someone said they were in hospital: they were in comas, and Marcio's wife had lost her baby. That turned out to be the truth.

If we hadn't got into the lift with those men waiting in the lobby, we would have gone to the thirteenth floor, and today I am sure we would be ashes. On that day we saw God has a plan for us.

To keep my mind busy I went back to work after about three weeks. All our friends have been really nice to us and they've never left us alone. We stayed at a very kind friend's house, and it was amazing because we could stay as a family. No money in the world could replace that friendship. [See Andreia's story in Chapter 9, pages 154–6.]

Since the second day, I have never cried for what I have lost. My husband and I were weeping together on the day after the fire and I said to him, 'We have lost everything!' But something inside me responded, *You have lost everything, but you still have everything, because you have your children.* From that moment I never complained again. We have more physical things now than we had before. Some of our friends who work for rich families spoke to their bosses and they sent clothes and items we needed. We have everything now.

My friends asked, 'Don't you miss your personal things?' and I replied, 'Of course there are personal things I will never have again, but they're only material things. What if I had all the jewellery, the kids' pictures and so on, but I had lost one member of my family?' I always think, *How many people would like to be in my shoes?* We were very, very lucky. We have our friends to support us. I saw people from the Tower who had no family, just strangers around to support them. We had friends coming from all over London. No money can buy that.

Jesus told us, 'Where your treasure is, there your heart is also.' I was asked, 'If you'd had half an hour, what would you have saved?', and I said, 'I brought what was most important for me: my children. My treasure is here.'

In the days after the fire the area was packed with people. I had no idea of what was going on outside because I stayed at my friends' flat all day. I went outside on Thursday afternoon. There were so many people. My daughter told me she had to go out because she was helping with donations. On that day we hadn't had any sleep for 24 hours and so it didn't register what she was doing.

Fatima's daughter Ines was an amazing example of calm and caring. She made the news when she went to take her GCSE Chemistry exam dressed in the clothes she escaped in, while the fire still burned. She achieved an A* grade in this exam. She then returned and got involved with sorting donations. Her father and brother also helped out. I asked Fatima if they went to get any things for themselves but she told me they only went to help out. Apparently at this point they didn't take anything for themselves except some washing-up liquid and a box of cereal! Later on they took the things they needed.

When I met the family, they were staying in temporary accommodation, a serviced apartment in High Street Kensington. Fatima admitted she would love to stay there. It was a very plush dwelling, tastefully furnished. She was pleased to tell me that all the furniture was theirs, ready to move when they bought their new home. She stressed:

God provides. As soon as I have my new place sorted I will be satisfied. We have been very fortunate. A lot of people who don't know us have been very kind. A friend's boss offered to pay for us to be in a hotel for a month, though we're just friends of his housekeeper, but we didn't accept his generosity as we were already staying in Andreia's flat.

Fatima was so quick to praise God in the situation:

> I felt a big chain of people around us, praying for us. A month after the fire my car was stolen from outside the hotel. My friends told me, 'It's not normal that you don't cry!' And I said, 'If I'm crying will it make any difference? My car won't come back! If I cry I will be more down and then I will have another problem on top of the others. I don't want to have depression. I had it in the past and I don't want it again. Whatever is gone is gone.'

Fatima's faith and trust in Jesus were very inspirational to me and I have subsequently shared her story frequently. She told me, 'We have finished this chapter and now we have a new one. I don't say to my friend, "I have a problem." Instead I tell my problem, "I have a friend [Jesus]."' This seems to be her amazing attitude to life. She told me that she is asking God what he wants her to do in the future. 'I want to be clay in [his] hands. We do our part and God does the rest.'

I doubt this is the last we'll hear of such an amazing woman.

Mr Abdurahman Sayed is chief executive of the Al Manaar Cultural Heritage Centre and Mosque. Exceptional interfaith relations have been a particular feature of this crisis. Many faiths have worked towards a common goal, and all have worked harmoniously together without tension or pride. From the first few hours many Muslims came with aid. The Al Manaar community centre was a hub of activity from the start. This is their story of being hope bearers for the community.

Mr Sayed has been involved in the local community for over 20 years. He used to live here and now he manages the organization of the community hub, both strategically and operationally, together with the day-to-day running of the Al Manaar Mosque. *Al manaar* means 'the lighthouse' in Arabic and in this crisis this has certainly been true. The mosque is hidden away from plain sight on Acklam Road, but despite that, it still attracts about 2,000 worshippers a week. Still more use the community hall or hire rooms. The day I visited, it was clear the community centre is used to welcoming non-Muslims, as the people with an appointment to see Mr Sayed just before me were also non-Muslims, and the community hall was hosting what looked like a corporate training day.

Mr Sayed is a very busy man, but he was courteous and exceptionally welcoming. Here is his story:

I awoke to a text from the caretaker informing me there was fire in a nearby building and requesting we offer shelter. I texted back, asking him to let everyone in: open the doors to Muslim and non-Muslim and make sure everyone is made welcome, give them any space they need. I told him I would be with him shortly. I also sent messages to my network and by the time I arrived at 8 a.m., already people were coming to volunteer, to donate and so on.

Worshippers worshipping here the night before were among the first people to go and try to help. When I arrived I saw four young girls standing outside. I thought they were from Grenfell Tower. I asked if they were from the Tower and needed anything, but they said, 'No, we just came to help.' I was so touched by that. They were young British girls, and I had no idea if they had any faith at all. Sometimes people make wrong assumptions about the young, assuming they [don't care] and are too much engaged in games and things, but the reality is they were the first four people I saw come to help.

I then met my colleagues. There were a few people from the Tower sleeping downstairs so we made sure they had the peace they needed. At this point I didn't even know what condition the Tower was in, so I thought maybe, as there were not many people at the mosque, I should take some supplies to them. It was Ramadan, so we had extra supplies of food and water because normally we cater for 250–300 people every evening. I tried to drive over with my seven-seater car full of supplies, but it was impossible to park near the building as it was all cordoned off. It's normally a five-minute drive but it took me over an hour and a half to get there.

When I got back I called the police and I asked if they could help me get supplies to the nearest centre, the Methodist church. They sent two officers who escorted me there. That was the first time I had entered that church and I found people dropping off supplies from the neighbourhood. I dropped off my supplies and I gave my card to anyone who I thought might be in charge, because I wasn't sure who was! I said, 'I'm from the Al Manaar Mosque and we're here to help. If you need any support, any supplies, we are here to help you.'

When I returned to the mosque, the road was congested with volunteers and supplies. This was beyond our greatest expectation and so immediately we cancelled our normal activities and started managing the situation. The phone was ringing non-stop. Luckily, we had some very good volunteers, some of whom were experienced managers, so they helped us by handling the phone calls and dealing with enquiries and the media. The credit really goes to them: they came from across the community, from different religions and ethnicities. Whatever boundaries people have in terms of belonging or affiliation, it went beyond all these things. They were also from across the nation. People brought supplies from as far as Manchester! There was a lot of support and suddenly we had turned ourselves into an emergency support centre! We also had survivors coming in to get the support they needed here.

Some people came to stay the night, both survivors and those visiting concerned relatives who were desperate to know what had happened to their family. After the second or third day the Council was housing people so our job became to provide support with supplies, pastoral care, financial assistance, clothing, toiletries and so on.

After three months the emergency phase was over and people were not in desperate need of supplies any more, but at the same time we had professional volunteers offering psychotherapy, counselling, emotional support, massage therapy and so on. We then became a hub where people could come, get support and relieve their stress. This service was extended to everyone in the community, because they were all affected by it. We thought this should be open to everyone, so we set up a counselling service here which is supported by the Council and the NHS. The unique aspect is that it combines the religious and cultural element with counselling and psychotherapy. We have it initially set up for a year but I think it will be a long-term thing. People come to see our imams but, although they have religious knowledge, such skills as counselling and diagnosing a problem may not be their area of expertise. To be able to offer the counselling service is useful, because then, if need be, people can be referred to the NHS and followed up accordingly.

It's normal for people of all faiths to use our buildings and community hall. We are unique in that our board of trustees always includes at least two non-Muslims from the Council who will be nominated to attend. Grenfell reinforced that principle. From the beginning all survivors were welcome here.

We have an open-door policy. We tried to give people space and not ask too many questions; better to risk one or two unscrupulous people than to put too much pressure on the survivors. There is a price to pay for everything.

One man who turned up was a white Englishman. We didn't want to ask him who he was, but we didn't know what he needed. I quietly asked him what he wanted, and he said some private space. We offered him a space downstairs and he said he'd be comfortable there. Then he asked for a candle. I asked one of my colleagues to go and buy him a candle. The colleague found him a candle and a lighter. The man lit the candle and then he started to worship. I knew he was a Christian because he made the sign of the cross. He kept worshipping silently. I stayed there to give him comfort and to see if he needed anything. He said 'Thank you, God', and that he felt much better. He had lost his brother in the fire and was looking for somewhere he could feel comfortable to worship. He had heard of Al Manaar and was happy to come here to pray for his brother. He then said, 'Thank you very much', and he left. I tried to offer him other things but he didn't want them. It was the first and last time I saw him, but I will never forget him. It made me feel very happy that this person chose this place to come and pray for his brother. You would imagine that he needed more support, but he just wanted some space where he felt comfortable.

The generosity we saw was above and beyond any human expectation. I think it must be within every individual's soul that when there is a crisis we need to come and help. The volunteers came from all different backgrounds, ages, men, women. All these people came together and no one paid attention to any differences. It was touching to see them all working together. It shows you this nation is really a generous nation.

My colleague and I were struggling because every time we tried to do something our phones would ring. One lady who works in the investment sector came to volunteer and we put her in the reception area with our phones either side of her, and for three days she was on the phone. She stayed till midnight every night. When we finally got to speak properly to her, she told us she was the vice chairman of an investment company. It shows people's dedication to volunteer. When we asked people to help they did it happily, cleaning or cooking. If you asked them their jobs you'd be surprised what they were, but everyone did whatever jobs they were asked without complaining.

The collective response, all these people coming and working together for a combined vision, was a huge thing for me. I became convinced that the whole issue of barriers and differences is artificial. Human beings have strong bonds, and values are universal. I saw this during the Grenfell crisis. There is something unique and strong in British society. Grenfell reinforces this unity.

We felt that we were doing the right thing by focusing on what the community needed and what they were telling us, and by trying to convey this to the media. My previous experience with the Council was always positive. They have been very supportive of the voluntary sector and of us at Al Manaar. Grenfell was not something we expected, but the lesson must be for all of us. We should not assume this will never happen again. Sometimes people compare us [favourably] to the Council because our response was so fast – we were on the ground very quickly – but my response is that it is different for us. For me, it took just a text message to open the door and issue instructions. For the Council there is bureaucracy to deal with and decision-making processes to go through.

There were shortcomings that I hope [the local authorities] will address. For example, there was a failure of leadership forthcoming when we asked for it. There was no mapping of where the resources were.

I think there will be a need for long-term counselling and a rehabilitation programme to help survivors to return to normal life. I met one man, a civil engineer, who lived on the twenty-first floor. He asked me, 'How am I going to start life again? Everything I have is gone.' How can ordinary people cope? We are hoping to conduct some research to see what is most appropriate and needed in the community.

I commented on how similar the work at Al Manaar was to that at the ClementJames Centre. Mr Sayed observed:

After the Grenfell fire, we started to get to know each other. Grenfell brought us together, not just to deal with the immediate situation, but also looking beyond. We hope to work together and coordinate our activities in a more organized fashion. The good news is that the Rugby Portobello [a local charity and community centre] has just raised funds for two support workers, one of them located at the ClementJames and the other at Al Manaar.

9

Hope bearers

A 'hope bearer' is a concept that I discovered when speaking with Ruth Divall, a lady who has completed a dissertation on hope. This struck a chord with me as I chatted to people who were helping others in great pain and struggling with the turmoil that the fire caused. When I asked them, 'What hope have you seen?' most of them responded, 'Very little!' They have spent time fighting political battles, helping families beat the memories that haunt them, and have seen people continuing to live in hotels months after the fire. They are worn out by their expenditure of love and care but they still continue to serve people, to represent them and counsel them. 'This is hope in action – this is Jesus!' Ruth says.

It occurred to me that although these people could not see it, they in fact were hope bearers. They were a source of hope to the suffering people, who needed someone to stand up for them or even just a listening ear. In Romans 12.15 Paul calls for us to rejoice with those who rejoice, and mourn with those who mourn. These hope bearers have done just that. In some cases, this has meant that they cannot see the good they have done among all the suffering that still exists, but it doesn't make it any less powerful or important! Ruth says:

Being Jesus in that situation is sitting and crying with people. We are meant to be interdependent, *not* happiness-seeking independent people. This is John Wyatt's thinking: 'Humankind by design is frail and interdependent and suffering is part of this experience.' [John Wyatt, *Matters of Life and Death*, Nottingham: IVP, 2009]

Our hope bearers will know, intuitively, that hope is a big part of suffering and the healing that follows it. We must not downplay suffering in a giddy search to feel better. Ruth says:

Soelle cautions us against minimizing suffering by looking for meaning and hope. I love the idea of lament where we rage with others against suffering! Hope must not stamp on suffering but it does need to open the door for healing. [Dorothee Soelle, *Suffering*, Philadelphia: Fortress Press, 1984]

These hope bearers are standing in the doorway, holding the door open for hope to enter.

When we are far off, the light at the end of the tunnel is very small, but I am certain these amazing people must believe that there is a light to aim for, or they would not be walking this tough path, trying to help people get justice or recovery. Ruth comments:

There is something our souls are hoping for . . . Hope keeps us going. Christian hope moves us forward because God is with us. God is walking with us through the suffering. This is the message of the cross. Christ descended to be with us in our pain. This has the power to keep us alive.

All Christians can be hope bearers, as indeed can those who aren't Christians. It's partly about showing resilience, and as Ruth says, 'Resilience can be key to a hopeful personality.' When we try to make the world a better place, we subscribe to hope. God can transform everything in the light of eternity. Sometimes, we don't see transformation in the here and now. When we hope for things for others, we can introduce them to new possibilities and the God who transforms. This transformation sometimes looks like acceptance and peace while walking through troubled times.

Jackie Blanchflower and the Latymer Community Church team

Jackie Blanchflower is the first hope bearer I spoke to. She and her husband Simon lead Latymer Community Church, one of the first response centres. They have been part of the community for over 20 years and Jackie was Secretary of the Residents' Association at the time of the fire. They have partnered with the Message Trust to see an Eden team established in Ladbroke Grove. The church has served tirelessly in the community, running events like an annual free Funday on Waynflete Square which is well loved and eagerly anticipated. The church prays, gives, and loves the community, and when the spotlight on the area has faded, it will still be here.

Speaking 14 weeks after the fire, Jackie said:

People are all at different stages of loss and bereavement.
In some ways it is hard to have a story of hope before you
have moved on. There are lots of good things that have
happened, but is that hope? For me, hope is the big
picture. My ultimate hope is that God is at work in this
and that he will bring some sort of restoration and
redemption out of it, but in terms of hope right now, it is
really hard.

There were lots of brilliant stories of people coming
together and seeing the good in people, like in every
disaster, but then you start getting the fracturing of the
community. This is the reality of our new brokenness. The
pain and loss make everything difficult, so rather than
holding on to the spontaneous unity we saw immediately
after the fire, people go back into their little enclaves.

Very early on we were looking for a saviour, someone to
come along and rescue us and make it all look better.
However, as Christians, we know that only God can do
that. I do have hope in the sense that some of the people
who have come here to help us are really committed to
helping us get through this. People here have all sorts of
questions about authority and the local government, Red
Cross, NHS . . . Trust is the key thing. I do think there
are some good people around, but it's going to be
results-dependent, because you have to rebuild trust.

Local residents have found they can trust the churches, and the community organizations have risen up and cared for the community. People have come forward to help out. We had about 100 people to our Residents' Association General Meeting after the fire, whereas normally if we had 20–30 attend an open committee meeting we'd feel we'd had a good turnout. People want to engage, but of course they also have their own agendas. My hope is that people will be able to come together and work to channel their anger, frustration and energy into something good.

For me the worst of [this tragedy] was that people predicted it, and it happened. That's what is so awful. I want to know: who is going to provide services where the residents are the focus and the service is for them, not part of a business? We are experiencing symptoms of a much bigger picture that is happening nationwide, but it is highlighted here. My hope is that this will be a pivotal turning point in social housing and that social policy will change as a result, but I fear this may be wishful thinking.

We need change quickly but these things take time. People need things now. It's hard to prejudge the inquiry and the criminal investigation. At the moment, there are lots of things that people say and think but are they actually the truth? I realize that I only see a very small part of anything that goes on. Who can judge? I have hope because God will move in this situation, but God alone can sort this out.

Jackie always has time for the most vulnerable in society. She treats people in a way that gives them dignity and respect. Jackie and her team are hope bearers who continually take the light of hope into dark places, and this gives others hope for themselves, that they are worthy of respect.

Zoe LeVack and Kids on the Green

Children's mental health was a high priority after the fire. The size of the Tower meant that no one could escape seeing it and so it was a constant reminder of what had happened for the whole community. Many different organizations provided activities for children in order to provide an alternative focus for them. One of these was called Kids on the Green (KOTG). Its members managed to get a circus-style marquee and it was set up in the open air on a local green space. This space was previously used only for dog-walking! The project provided after-school activities and fun for children in the wake of the fire.

Zoe struck me as a hope bearer as she shared her heart and passion for children and young people in general. She wants to provide them with healthy choices for their lives. She works to give youth a chance for a better future than they might think is possible. Zoe is the powerhouse behind Kids on the Green, a project that hundreds of children, including my own, have enjoyed since June 2017. Here is her story:

Kids on the Green started on 14 June 2017. I'm a local youth worker and came down to the area as quickly as I could. I spent most of the morning sorting through donations at the Edward Woods Community Centre, and then took half an hour lunch break. I ended up wandering up Latimer Road and was really shocked at how it was just like a war zone. I was particularly upset by the number of children and young people who were milling around there without any obvious parental supervision, looking completely devastated. On my way back I realized it was an ideal place to set up an emergency response unit, to lure the children away from Latimer Road, which was just such a scene of hell.

It was horrific. I approached the head of UPG [Urban Partnership Group], which is the charity based at the Edward Woods Community Centre, and asked if I could gather a team and pop up a project the next day. I had their trust as I'd worked with them before, and they agreed.

We posted on social media that we wanted child-centred practitioners to help us. We especially asked for a mental health practitioner. Within half an hour we had a sports coach, a psychotherapist and a primary school teacher who had been on a teaching break. We had a bag of footballs and a box of felt-tip pens and we took some water, some crisps that had been donated, a table, and off we went.

I went off on my bike and gave out handwritten fliers. There was no thought in the name – it was the first thing that came to me: 'Kids on the Green'. I rescued a bunch of teenagers from some journalists and they were our first customers.

I'd set up an emergency response project the previous year, ironically in the same space, in response to the murder of a local teenager who was stabbed to death on the Portobello. There were a lot of very angry young men and I was worried that there would be a huge retaliation, as the summer holidays were approaching and there is usually an increase in youth violence. I worked with them through the summer and there was no retaliation.

No one could have predicted how Kids on the Green developed. We thought it was going to happen for three days, then it was a week, then two weeks, then we thought it needed to carry on. In August we applied for money from the London Funders and were given £10,000, and Love for Latimer – the brilliant DJ Stuart Patterson and his friends – gave us £14,000. I'm very fortunate to have amazing volunteers and a very strong core group of staff who are great and who work for much less than they should.

Zoe's phone rings. She asks someone to take the call, and says to me in a stage whisper, 'Someone's given us a minibus!' These kinds of offers have become a regular event for her team and they joyfully use everything they are given. She continues:

We've had quite a few people donating privately and some of those donations have come with really lovely stories. A primary school in Devon sent us £300, and you know, every penny of that was from kids making cupcakes or selling bookmarks. It's heart-warming to know that people all over the country wish you well.

I chose to do certain media requests, *BBC Breakfast* and LBC [talk radio], and as a result of that we got even more support for the project. Publicity can be something you can use to your advantage. In some instances the media have behaved badly around Grenfell, but I also get disheartened when I don't see anything about Grenfell, because I want the rest of the country to know what's going on down here. It's not appropriate to flaunt children's abject grief but also we've got to keep this story alive because we haven't had any justice yet. We need the rest of the country to know what an appalling situation we have to cope with and that it should never happen again and that lessons are learnt and people are kept accountable. We must see prison sentences.

I have heard a lot of sad stories, heartbreaking stories. Children are beginning to talk now. To start with, there was a lot of very sad artwork, but now they just want to talk about it all the time. Sometimes you go home and have a good cry. The children ask funny questions so you see that they are processing things, asking what their dead friend's bedroom looks like now, for example. One youth said to me, 'Many of us don't want to use the youth clubs any more because it reminds us of all our dead friends we used to go with.' How would I have coped, as a 13-year-old, losing so many of my mates in that way and watching it happen?

One little girl picked up a hoola-hoop. As she started to hoola she began to talk about her friend who had died. Her mum thanked us because she hadn't spoken about it and she'd been trying to get her to open up. There she was, quite lackadaisically hoola-hooping and talking about her friend. It unlocked something inside for her. Circus skills seem to be really therapeutic for children, which is why we always try to include them. Some of the most positive comments we have had are from the mums, saying, 'Thank you for KOTG because it's given us a chance to get to know our neighbours through a collective grieving process, bringing people together who have never met or perhaps have been past each other a hundred times but never spoken. Grenfell has united everybody. Having Kids on the Green, with everyone sharing common experiences, helps us to understand other women from different faiths and backgrounds.' The Muslim community and the non-Muslim community on Edwards Woods have integrated a bit more, which has been great.

Kelly Markna, a local resident, originally from Estonia, lives near the green and so it was a natural place for her to take her children after school and during the holidays. She says:

It started about a week after the fire. They set up a place
for people to go. It was a peaceful place to be, with
activities for the kids and therapists and activities done by
different people for the children. I first went there the first
few days it started. I don't know what I would've done
without it. Being there, you could speak to other people or
you could just sit while the kids were playing. It was one
place where you could just be.

The daily activities on offer changed according to the people
who came to volunteer. It was like a lucky dip and there was
always something new and exciting happening. Kelly remembers:

There were different sports, football, boxing gloves and
hula-hoops. It had art therapists, and different people
came in. There were lots of volunteers and then at one
point they had a circus artist and a bubble man. There
were homeopaths, some people came to do massage, and
the first few weeks there was pizza at the end of the day
and sometimes they had some other foods, always snacks
and drinks. In the last couple of weeks they had takeaway
fried chicken for the whole group, for 20 or 30 kids.

Kelly enjoyed it for several reasons:

You just become friends with these people because you
would see them every day. It was a place to go. I don't

think I actually spoke about Grenfell once. I made quite a few friends there. There was a lady, called Nadia, who is actually an ice skater, who used to come and do artwork with the kids. She came all the way from Guildford and she and I became very friendly. There were teachers coming during the holidays too.

Kids on the Green also participated in the Notting Hill Carnival. Kelly says, 'I think the reason KOTG did the Carnival was so that people didn't forget about Grenfell.'

As well as the Carnival, Kids on the Green organized a free weekend away at Woodrow High House in Amersham. This is a residential activity centre with extensive facilities.

Kelly, along with many others, enjoyed Kids on the Green because of the sense of community:

It was really nice to see our green space being used, with everyone being together, not just the green space sitting empty and people doing their own thing. It was the first time since I've been in London that I've seen the community meeting up and talking to each other. Now you know your neighbours when you used to just walk past them. I can't walk around without knowing someone to say 'hello' to.

Kids on the Green has continued to run throughout the autumn and winter in an indoor venue, but the group left the green at the end of September. They left on a high with a bouncy castle and a visit from an exotic animals petting zoo. My son Caleb was delighted to meet a caiman, a skunk and a baby boa constrictor!

Total Family Coaching and Parenting

Shivata Thind, Adelina Badivuku and their colleagues from Total Family Coaching and Parenting are also hope bearers. They are a community-based service that works with vulnerable members in the area, especially refugees, helping them with their parenting in the light of loss and trauma. They operate from below the Harrow Club, a few hundred metres from the Tower.

I spoke to Shivata, a parenting specialist and family coach, who told me a part of their story. 'As a local service we realized we were ideally placed to help during Grenfell,' she said. 'We came across a flier for Kids on the Green and we offered intervention for the parents.'

They have been regular faces at Kids on the Green but their work for Grenfell survivors did not stop there. Shivata explained:

We are offering services during the night at the hotels, after parents have put their children to bed. It's a listening service for anyone who is anxious and needs someone to talk to out of hours. We open from 8 p.m. to 3 a.m. We offer a safe space, a therapeutic approach towards healing. We wait for the right time to work with people, but we can work with them as soon as they are ready.

People can talk about not just Grenfell. Some are refugees and have lots to talk about from before Grenfell, so it's nice for them to be able to map that out in a safe space, either to find some solutions or to find a way to deal with their concerns in a more positive and helpful way.

Parents who don't have great mental health to start with [may not be] able to parent their children in an effective way. This perpetuates problems because they know their children are traumatized and they [may not be] able to install boundaries because they are overcompensating for the fact that the children are traumatized. Yes, Grenfell was tragic but you still need to parent, and you don't need to overcompensate for the fact that the children are grieving and so are you. We have been able to help parents deal with their own stuff and then, through that, help their children. What we do ties in beautifully with Kids on the Green because we are offering sessions there, doing one-to-ones and group work.

Shivata and Adelina have been a quiet but constant story of Grenfell Hope. They have been hope bearers, in the darkest parts of the night, to those who have been directly affected, the survivors and their children, and they have sat and supported those who are trying to return to normal life.

Shivata says:

The greatest thing in terms of hope is this: the trauma could have led to people staying indoors alone, but instead families are coming and accessing services because they have built trust and established links with people they may not have necessarily spoken to before, for example at Kids on the Green. Building those friendships has allowed them to think, *Actually I can deal with this!*

Please pray for Shivata and Adelina as they continue to do such front-line work.

Howard Taylor and his team from the ClementJames Centre

Howard, who works at the ClementJames Centre, says:

Despite the fire being a terrible tragedy, it did highlight the pre-existing sense of community in North Kensington, which showed strength and unity throughout. My team have rallied together, balancing their normal roles with our Grenfell response, offering a listening ear, advice and guidance, processing funds and ensuring that no task is too big to support those in need.

The area is getting recognition for its incredible sense of community. People are also now taking note of what support and services are missing in the area and trying to set these up. This will support and develop the local area as a whole. The Grenfell survivors themselves always show an incredible sense of calm and respect, even when in frustrating meetings and facing daily challenges. In the days immediately following, the Entertainer toy company and Marks & Spencer were pivotal in helping us sort and move donations to where they were needed.

Father Alan Everett, Howard and the ClementJames team have borne so much hope for others as they have sought funding, grants and donations, and tried to ensure these things go to the right places. Their workload increased dramatically after Grenfell, yet they persevered.

A minha casa é a sua casa – *Andreia's story*

Andreia lives near Latimer Road tube station, within a few moments' walk of the Tower. She is Portuguese, and knew several Spanish and Portuguese families who lived in the Tower. She recalls, 'When my mum woke me to tell me what was happening she said, "It's Fatima's building on fire!"' (See Fatima's story in Chapter 8, pages 123–30.) All of the families that Andreia knew escaped safely, although tragically the youngest child, Gomez, was stillborn as a direct result of the smoke.

Andreia was involved in helping in various relief efforts, but the main thing she did was an act of total self-giving. Here is her story:

> In the first few days there was a lot of confusion about where people should go after the fire, and Fatima and her family went to stay with some other friends. I'd been following how they were doing and what was happening to them quite closely and, by the second day, when there still wasn't anything in place for them, I suggested that

they come and stay in my flat. It was also a convenient location because they could be close to everything.

Initially I thought we could all stay there together, but when they arrived and I saw what they looked like and how they were, I thought they needed some time out as a family. Basically they needed some privacy. They play quite a big part in the Portuguese church and the Portuguese community so they were being inundated with phone calls and people turning up randomly with stuff to give them and to make sure that they were all right. But I just saw a family who had been through the most horrendous experience and who needed sanctuary.

I had the option to go and stay with my parents who only live ten minutes up the road, so I offered them my flat. I pretty much packed a couple of large carrier bags, some with my stuff and some with my daughter's, not even thinking long term. I just grabbed some stuff and tried to leave them to it.

I didn't give much thought to how long we would need to stay away, until my daughter said, 'When can we go back to our house?' I hadn't fully appreciated quite how disruptive the situation could be for her. I had assumed it was just going to be for a couple of weeks. It turned into six or seven.

I did start to feel the strain of not being in my own home after a while and living out of plastic bags. I had to nip back a few times to get more things, which of course they didn't mind. I'm glad I did it because I think it gave them a bit of space and it also gave them an opportunity that I don't think many people had, in the sense of being able to start building up their life again. They had a place to put things. They could get suitcases from the centres and fill them with clothes or food – not only for themselves but for other people too. One family we know were hospitalized, and the daughters and mother remained in induced comas for nearly four weeks and so my friend Fatima started collecting items for them and their daughters. So initially when I was walking into my house for the first couple of weeks it was floor-to-ceiling boxes! Then everything started getting sorted out. That was quite nice to see, that it was not just one family being helped.

Many people were keen to share their homes but few offers were accepted. Andreia's generosity for so many weeks allowed her friends space to regroup and work out in privacy what they wanted, and also enabled them to cook their own food, not relying on hotel catering. Andreia has been a hope bearer by offering all that she had to her friends.

There are many other hope bearers who continue to work, mostly unnoticed and unappreciated, but the impact of their deeds is part of the beautiful picture of healing that is being created in ugly circumstances. They have worked tirelessly and selflessly to bring light to others and a hope for the future. Each of their stories touched me and gave me something to reflect on in my own life.

Hope bearers are always needed.

10

The world was watching

Julia Samuels, a grief counsellor who came to help at Grenfell, and a friend of the late Princess Diana, said:

> The Grenfell Tower tragedy has really shaken me. There is something about the scale of it, the speed of it, the unstoppable destruction of so many lives and families on a normal evening, that it is hard to comprehend, and I continue to feel the fear of it . . . Yet the kindness of strangers, neighbours, even people from different countries is the one aspect of this devastating tragedy that can give us hope.
>
> (*Telegraph Magazine*, 26 August 2017)

Cornwall Hugs Grenfell – holidays of hope

One lady who was watching the television news from her home in beautiful Cornwall was deeply affected by the fire and was moved to take action. Esmé Page created the Cornwall Hugs Grenfell holidays. Interviewing Esmé was, for me, like opening a shoebox and discovering it was full of gold. I thought I was doing a fairly basic interview, but an hour later I was inspired and encouraged by what I had heard.

Esmé modestly mentioned that she likes to be organized and make things happen. It seemed her entire career path up to that point had prepared her perfectly for what lay ahead. Here is her story:

When I saw the television report about the fire, I was particularly affected by the words of the London fire commissioner, Dany Cotton, talking about her concerns for the emotional well-being of her firefighters. I was really struck by the fact that a woman was heading up the capital's Fire Service and also that she was willing to say that. [The Grenfell disaster] was something way beyond the experience of the Fire Brigade in London. That, coupled with some of the interviews with survivors and the people who lived around and seeing what they were facing, made me realize what a journey of healing everybody was going to be on and what an enormous wound in the community the fire had created.

The idea for Cornwall Hugs Grenfell was immediately there, as if it had been downloaded into my head. I thought, *They are going to need respite, space, peace and hope.* The main thing I felt, looking at the television footage, was just how hopeless the whole situation was. The building was still burning and there was a severe lack of information. Clearly more people were going to be dead than it was possible to know at that time. It was going to scar hundreds of people – the firefighters, the survivors, people all around the community.

If I put my mind to do something I generally do it, but not like this. I have never gone out on a limb before. I spoke to my husband and one other person about this, but what I planned was a massive task and a logistical nightmare. How would we connect with the people who needed [some respite and space]? How would we make sure they were the right people? Would other people offer their property? It was one enormous tangle of spaghetti. But it didn't go away.

On the Sunday, I went swimming in the sea near Porthcurno. The sea was a beautiful turquoise, absolutely stunning. That is where I felt convicted. It wasn't a voice but it was a pretty strong thought: 'Who are you *not* to do this? These people have to have this, the nourishing and healing environment of Cornwall, the beauty and the sensory antidote that is the Cornish landscape. They need to see the sea and to look up and see a horizon [which, to me, felt totally absent every time I saw the television coverage]. Everything they see is a constant reminder of the trauma and of the loss.' I felt as if God was saying, 'I want them to have this. This is my creation and they need this.'

This is not normal for me. I am usually [sceptical about] those who say 'God told me', because how would they know? How can you be sure? It felt very clear to me, but risky. So many things were unknown. It was as if I was stepping out across a chasm where there was no bridge.

What I have found is that everything we have needed has been made available. There has been a most immense provision and it has been a team effort all the way through.

The night before it started I prayed, 'If this is what you want me to do, you will provide, so over to you, God.' I posted a message on my personal social media page asking for accommodation. Within 24 hours we had over 100 offers of property. I realized within an hour I had to learn how to create a community page to move people on to that. It was instantly unmanageable. Within ten days we had a proper website that people could register on. All kinds of things happened, showing God's effectiveness.

I decided I was going to have to make it good enough, not the best! I had to be pragmatic. Within six weeks we had our first family down to Cornwall. People came throughout the summer. Five months after the fire, we have had 175 people down. That's over 1,200 holiday days. Over 1,000 people have been involved in some way from Cornwall. Either they have been part of a business which has contributed, or they have given some money, or volunteered to accompany a group. Around 150 businesses have contributed too.

We have offered two kinds of holiday. One is an individual holiday let. The other is a structured group holiday which has activities you can join in. It has trips and excursions but also therapeutic elements like massage, meditation, singing workshops, art or sculpture workshops for people with PTSD [post-traumatic stress disorder]. It's a structured environment within which you can access other activities.

The main client groups are firefighters and their families, who can only access the individual holiday lets, and the Grenfell group. The Grenfell group are made up of Tower survivors, those from the evacuated blocks and those who are bereaved, and support workers in need of a break, and they can access both types of holiday.

What we offer is something very simple. I wanted it to be respectful and simply offer peace, respite and hope. We want to give people time to be a family, and to make new memories, especially for children to have new family memories so they have them to help with resilience. We call it a 'suitcase of new memories' that they can get out at any time to nourish them. They have all got a suitcase of hideous memories and images already, plus, just like all of us, our clients generally didn't start from a perfectly happy basis. People already had cancer, people were already bereaved of a parent this year, people had just lost their jobs or were struggling to make ends meet. It's an amazingly resilient population but they had faced many difficult situations prior to the fire.

The respite of being out of London W11 has been invaluable in itself. Back there, people are continually ambushed by the Tower as they walk around. Families have changed their routes to school to prevent their children seeing pictures of their dead friends on the memory walls. To see nothing to remind you is a rest for the mind, the eyes and the soul.

We have seen peace, hope and love here. People have received so much love from Cornwall, but it has been a figure of eight: it has blessed Cornwall as much as Kensington. Business leaders have stepped forward to say how much it has enriched them and their team, and it has been a cross-faith enterprise – Christians, people of no faith, Muslims who have come. It's always been about love and it has been really authentic.

From such an extreme place of loss, there is no space for any pretence. That fits too, because Cornwall is not really a place of pretence. It's beautiful, but it's tough to live here. People work hard to make a living, and they live by the sea so they know about loss, tragedy and community. They just bring themselves. So you have this community of love and understanding, people who share themselves and their lives.

It was very moving seeing Hanan Wahabi, a survivor from the ninth floor, and her daughter Sara enjoying kayaking together. Sara had spoken about how she hadn't seen Mummy smile for so long. I was so impressed by Hanan's commitment to her daughter as, despite her grief, she threw herself into the activities.

Extraordinary acts of courage and sacrifice have been performed by the parents in getting the children to go on holiday. They didn't know what they were coming to or who we were, but they still caught the train at 7.06 a.m. from Paddington and came.

Before the fire they felt unseen, ignored. They had to apply and beg and justify everything. What this project has done is this: they have felt *seen*, in their grief and their loss and their situation; they have felt valued and loved for who they are. They haven't had to justify themselves or qualify for anything. I suppose that's the nature of unconditional love: to be seen, valued, loved and accepted. It's an antidote to their overall experience.

We have committed to keep going until 2019. Having a holiday in the future is like having hope on the horizon and we want to see this through. There are probably nearly 400 people who still want to come. It's been at such breakneck speed. It's not a Christian organization – anyone can contribute and anyone can receive – but the way it happened so fast, and the way I got over my fears, were thanks to God.

Just before the last group arrived, I was exhausted. They were due to arrive in two days. I was praying, and *plop*: I saw an image of a blonde, attractive woman. I felt God saying, 'I've got this young woman who is going to be with you for the whole week. She can help you.' Volunteers come to help throughout the week, but up until then I'd been the only volunteer actually in residence all week long on these group trips. It's an enormous amount to handle on your own. I emailed a few people, asking them if they knew who this blonde woman might be because it felt like God might be sending her. It was ridiculous to think someone might be free with two days' notice, but within 24 hours someone contacted me who happened to be blonde. She came and stayed for the whole week and she was incredible. When things got tough I just sent her off to pray. I've recruited people before in business, but what was unusual was that she was available and God gave me complete peace that we would get on fine and I wouldn't need to continually check up on her.

Six-month anniversary service at St Paul's Cathedral

On the six-month anniversary of the fire Bishop Graham Tomlin and the staff of St Paul's Cathedral arranged a service to remember those who died and support those who are still suffering, those who lived in the Tower and those who lost loved ones, and those in the local community. The service was aired live on the BBC and was attended by Prince Charles and Camilla, the Duke and Duchess of Cambridge, Prince Harry, as well as Prime Minister Theresa May, Jeremy Corbyn, the current leader of the Labour party, singers Adele and Marcus Mumford, and some other celebrities.

The service was multifaith and diverse, including contributions from Ebony, the steel pan band, and the Salvation Army Brass band alongside the St Paul's Cathedral choir. Children from some of the local schools came and laid green hearts at the foot of a specially commissioned banner commemorating Grenfell. Bishop Graham preached a sermon about hope, but he also brought out some of the hard truths and pain of those who still suffered, many of whom longed to be, but were not yet, permanently housed.

For me, the most striking part of the service was the end, when those who had lost a close friend or family member walked out of the cathedral carrying white roses or photos of their loved ones. There were hundreds: it seemed as if the line would never end. It was a tangible sign of how many people's lives had been torn apart by that terrible night.

Creative outpourings of grief and solidarity

The media interest has been exceptionally high and there are several documentaries being made about the fire. Gaby Aung, a producer working for Minnow Films, has become a familiar face in the community as she has been working to tell the story. She explained her approach:

We want to make a lasting documentary that remembers those who tragically lost their lives, and also gathers the testimony of the people who survived, the bereaved families, and those who were in positions of responsibility before, during and after the fire. Reflecting the strength and spirit of the local community is also of huge importance to us. We hope this film represents an opportunity to bring the experiences of those so deeply affected to the attention of the wider public. I have been very inspired and affected by the people I have met and testimonies I have heard from the local community, and out of this great tragedy and sadness I have also witnessed incredible humanity.

Minnow Films has made many award-winning documentaries in the past. Their ethos is to be thought-provoking while making films of high quality, and I hope this film will tell the story faithfully.

Images of the Tower will become iconic in the story of this neighbourhood. As images have been powerful in displaying the horror of the building, images have also been part of the healing of the area. As an area that you could refer to as a 'hood' (neighbourhood), graffiti has always been important, but street art has now proliferated. These are not just tags and swear words written by angst-ridden teens! Grown-ups come to the wall under the Westway flyover and paint their pictures, their statements and their stories. I've never been certain whether it is legal or not, but it happens, and sometimes the effects have been very moving. Graffiti tells stories about how people are feeling and what they care about.

There is something very biblical about this, as Deuteronomy 6.9 talks about writing the words of God's law on the door frames of your house. Graffiti seems to be a modern way of doing this!

The graffiti began to be part of the expression of public attitude in the face of the confusion. There were two-metre-high letters saying 'Smile', there were spray-painted pictures of Grenfell Tower with angels' wings flying to heaven, and there were all the voices crying out for justice and making their public comments, and requesting answers to their questions.

One piece that really struck me said, in metre-high letters, 'We are one'. I wondered: in what respects are we one? We are all human. We are united in grief in all the different forms it takes. We are united in our horror of what happened. We are living in an area that now has a terrible reputation for pain and anguish. This is very sacred language. Christians are one in Christ. We are one body because we all share the same bread, the communion of Jesus, because Jesus united us in his death. Somehow the suffering united people in a way that was different from and deeper than we had ever experienced before.

The Truth Wall

Under the Westway (that is, under the A40 flyover) there is an area behind the fantastic Indian takeaway which has previously been a bit of a no-go area at night. During the day, it was a walkway – nothing more. But the transformation is unbelievable! This has become a vibrant hub of the community and undergone a complete change, from a large puddle under the Westway to a friendly outdoor living space, known as the Truth Wall. Due to its direct view of the Grenfell Tower it was a place where people stopped to look at the Tower as they walked under the Westway. Simultaneously others were starting to paint and write words of encouragement, anger, frustration and sadness on the walls, pillars and floor in this area. The graffiti artists needed somewhere to sit, and those who wanted to contemplate the Tower also appreciated a seat. So members of the Truth Wall team have built seating from old furniture, boards and pieces of rubbish that they have made beautiful. They have planted a garden with flowers in a disused flower bed – guerrilla gardening is clearly a new craze! An offshoot of this, The Olive Branch Charity, is now functioning and creating green spaces for peace and reflection to bring positivity to the community.

One of the Truth Wall team members commented:

The best thing that has happened is that different people have come together and we've learnt not to judge anybody. Everyone has a different story. Everybody has worked together for the same one thing. The area was dirty, and now when you see people walking past, all of a sudden their faces light up because they see the flowers and it's all bright. Then they see the piano and they run towards it and start playing. We get all kinds of people from all walks of life playing the piano. It's been amazing. The Truth Wall was a naturally evolving thing. It is such an open space. It is almost like a family – you find lots of different vulnerable people coming here. It's a place of non-judgement and it's warm and welcoming. Other people who have suffered trauma gravitate to the area. It's a safe place and they come from other places and keep staying and staying and join in. If you want to leave you can just walk away. People often walk past before stopping, then gradually worm their way in, or they just stop and play the piano.

This was not a project that had a start or end point. 'I can't see any end vision but it's an ever-evolving space,' said another team member. 'It's important to keep it evolving and flowing and getting the community down there and bringing them all together.'

Those who have problems with authority and being enclosed have found a welcome in this open space. It is somewhere where hospitality is always offered on your own terms. One of the team told me of a visit from a man who suffered with schizophrenia; for him, just seeing the Tower brought on a very extreme reaction. Two of the team prayed for him and this was a real comfort to him. The team is not affiliated to any faith or group or race, but their actions happened to meet the need of a hurting person. It is easy to see Jesus among these vulnerable people as they meet and try to make sense of the broken parts of their lives. The authorities are probably not keen for them to be there, but the Truth Wall team are reaching people who may have nowhere else to go, or perhaps are unable to connect with the usual methods of help and support.

Bunting

Along the railings around Latimer Road and Silchester Road are some beautiful art pieces. Yellow ribbons are a popular sign of solidarity, and many people have used them to remember the missing and dead at Grenfell. The trees have been tied with yellow ribbons by local people, but this seems to have started an avalanche. Knitting groups from all over the world have encouraged one another to send in knitted yellow bunting. The first piece I examined had been sent from Australia; it surprised and delighted me that people right around the world were thinking about us in such a special way. The bright colour also focuses your eyes on the bunting and not on the burnt-out building.

Stars of HOPE

A similar project is Stars of HOPE. Some of the railings in the area have been decked like Christmas trees since late June 2017. They have home-painted stars hanging from them, and an attached message says:

> Stars of HOPE empowers children of all ages to transform individuals and communities in need of hope through the power of art and messages of healing. These Stars of HOPE were made by the students at Bodine High School for International Affairs, Pennsylvania, USA, Pulse Nightclub, Orlando, Florida, and employees of SunGard USA to let the people of Manchester and London know that we are thinking of you and that you are not alone. Stars of HOPE has been to 150 communities and 24 countries.

One star that I liked said 'Hope is forever'. These messages are amazing gestures from people who may never even visit London but have felt our pain.

#24hearts

A project known as #24hearts started with the aim of using various art materials to make one heart for each of the 24 floors of the Grenfell building and displaying them. People of all ages were able to take part and soon the hearts were complete. However, the organizers didn't stop there as it was such a great project.

The project is based at Maxilla Gardens, just north of the Westway. I went there with a friend one day and we created a large heart in the Grenfell 'tube' design with our combined six children. There were 200 hearts overall, created and hung along the carnival route so that everyone who visited Carnival in 2017 could see them. Before Christmas, #24hearts asked children in local schools to draw portraits of people who were special to them, and the best pictures were made into banners that were hung near Ladbroke Grove tube station. The project continues . . .

Humanity responds to suffering

So often, the suffering that we hear of is far removed from us. It appears for a second on a screen in a news bulletin, then it's gone and the next flash of horror is revealed. But people all around the world, through their thoughtful gestures, have ensured that this is not so for Grenfell. The human interest, the culpability of the authorities, and the size of the police investigation (the second biggest ever in the UK after the 7/7 London bombings) all remind the public that there is a community in Kensington that is suffering and this is not a problem that will go away. These reminders mean that politicians can be kept accountable for their grand words. Justice will mean that people follow through and their words become deeds (although the authorities might need nudging). When they choose to, members of the press have a long memory that can be utilized for good.

The press can't go unmentioned. Newspeople have been at times helpful and at times excruciating. Suffering people have been hounded for comment and stories. There have been so many violations of people's privacy and dignity. I myself have found it tempting to push too far, to ask one too many questions or even to pursue the wrong person, for all of which I am penitent. However, those working in the media have been in many cases insensitive, publishing information about people without their express permission and often getting it wrong. I was interviewed on the monthly Silent March for Grenfell by a journalist with an agenda, someone who wanted to press her point of view and not listen to mine. The problem with the media is that journalists need an immediate story. What would be more interesting would be to speak to people when they have had a chance to recover and reflect, and this might mean the story is told in three years' time, but our society pushes for it now. Those who were helping often got interrupted in their tasks by journalists asking them for comment. Surely it is more important to leave people to do their tasks? Those with a certain political agenda have sometimes used the situation to make their point. The key things this community wants are that such a tragedy should never happen again and that the investigation be thorough and honest.

What about us?

People all over the UK live in high-rise flats. The Grenfell tragedy has raised questions for them. Am I safe in my home? What would happen if my home caught fire? Would I have to face the same fate? As people ask themselves these questions, they are forced to speak up. They find that they no longer want to accept the supposition that they'll probably be safe in an accident. They want assurance that they and their family will be protected, and when it comes to safety, it's worth fighting about. Grenfell has acted as an omen of what is to come if we don't care for the needs of those in high-rise homes, and it is not a cost we should ever be prepared to pay again.

Camden Council listened to the warning of Grenfell and evacuated five high-rise tower blocks in the Chalcots Estate that contained 800 homes; the buildings had been clad by the same company as Grenfell. Georgia Gould, the council leader, said, 'All we care about is getting people to safety. The cost we can deal with later.' Only 83 residents refused to move out. People were moved to hotels and were lodged in a local sports centre. The *Guardian* newspaper reported the story:

'We realise that this is hugely distressing for everyone affected [said Councillor Gould] and we will be doing all we can,

alongside London fire brigade and other authorities, to support
our residents at this difficult time. The Grenfell fire changes
everything, we need to do everything we can to keep residents
safe' . . .

Tulip Siddiq, the Labour MP for Hampstead and Kilburn,
the constituency in which Chalcots is located, said the council
decision was the right thing to do.

'If you think someone's in danger, especially in light of
Grenfell, you take the first decision, even if it's not ideal. Off
the back of the meeting we had last night, in which lots of
residents raised concerns, Camden council and London fire
brigade did the right thing, which was to carry out the safety
checks . . . It may seem dramatic to some people, but if you are
in a position of responsibility then I think it's the right decision
to make.'   (*The Guardian*, 23 June 2017)

In listening to those in her ward, the councillor was setting an
example for others across the UK and around the world. It was
a terrible inconvenience for all parties involved to move so
many households out, but taking people seriously and caring
for them is a messy business and people are more important
than profit. It is another question altogether whether the works
carried out to make the blocks safe were done well enough. In
a rich country like the UK, where we have finances for nuclear
weapons, supposedly to keep us safe from invading nations, we
should equally be able to keep people safe in their own homes
from their own homes!

It wasn't just in the UK. In other countries, for example the United Arab Emirates (UAE), there were also concerns. New fire rules in the UAE were brought in during 2017. Pawan Singh reports that

> there remain potentially dozens, perhaps hundreds, of buildings with cladding that need to be inspected [in the UAE]. One mechanism to deal with this issue is to introduce a level of transparency into what cladding is used on which buildings, and allow the market to decide. (*The National*, 25 June 2017)

This is a good regulation, and the fact that other countries are looking at their safety policies in the light of Grenfell is revelatory. If people know what risks they are taking, they are free to make choices; the issues arise when people are not aware that they live with risk.

Suffering is something that every nation can understand. A biblical passage that is often used in weddings to denote unity in marriage includes the verse: 'A cord of three strands is not quickly broken' (Ecclesiastes 4.12b). This passage is actually about the pains of suffering alone and how, when people work together, they are stronger. If one strand is broken, the other two strands will hold the rope in place. The rope is damaged but it's still holding. This is an ideal picture of a suffering community. When one person trips, the others can catch him or her, but when we become dispersed we are weaker. This is perhaps why there have been so many protests, marches and public displays of unity during this time. They build the participants up and remind them to stay together. Imagine, though, if the whole world is watching and championing us! Then we will come through this time, not broken and forgotten, but strong and supported as the world hugs Grenfell.

11

From me to you

'For I know the plans I have for you,' declares the LORD, 'plans
to prosper you and not to harm you, plans to give you hope
and a future.'

(Jeremiah 29.11)

Why do I have hope in these dark times?

Some of my friends do not share my optimism. They think
the Council will revert to form, and people will be left festering
in hotels or inadequate accommodation. They don't think any
change has been made. They see the slaughter of their neighbours and they don't expect anyone to pay.

A common theme is that residents feel someone needs to
be held accountable for the horror they suffered and the
lives lost. To quote Hanan Wahabi (whose brother and family
died and who escaped with her children), speaking to
Jon Snow on the Channel 4 News, 'Is it bad for me to say I
think somebody needs to pay? A prison sentence needs to
happen.'

I believe in justice. Those who have done wrong should be
punished, especially if they wilfully deceived people and were
lazy about the safety of over 300 human beings. Some of those
in the spotlight are already suffering. *What if I had done some-*

thing I neglected to do? they may be thinking. *Would those lives have been saved?* For others, perhaps there is an attempt to escape the blame, to cover their tracks so their part in the disaster won't be discovered.

I would like to see a thorough investigation and I believe the police are doing that. It is a very large investigation and they are interviewing countless witnesses, including firefighters and survivors. However, justice is much more than a handful of people being arrested and imprisoned, or large fines being handed out to corporations. This will not help us sleep better in our beds, safe in the knowledge that the baddies have been caught. This is a much wider issue.

I believe in a justice that will probably not be seen on earth until Jesus returns. However, the Bible speaks of Jubilee, a year of justice for the poor and oppressed, when property is shared out. This is what we need. In a society where the rich are becoming astronomically wealthy, the poor are becoming worse off. In 1985 *Faith in the City*, a report by the Church of England on Urban Priority Areas, caused outrage among Conservative politicians by suggesting that Thatcherite policies caused poverty in the UK. Over 30 years later, sadly their words still ring true:

> Poverty is at the root of powerlessness. Poor people in UPAs are at the mercy of fragmented and apparently unresponsive public authorities. They are trapped in housing and in environments over which they have little control. They lack the means

and opportunity – which so many of us take for granted – of
making choices in their lives.   (*Faith in the City*, p. xv)

Rich people have choices; poor people have limits. The November
2017 UK budget was released with predictions that in the next
year poorer families would be £700 poorer and wealthier households would be £100 richer. The sum of £700 in poorer homes
represents food, clothing and heat. In a wealthier home, £100
works out at about one extra takeaway coffee a week.

The tenets of a civilized society are food, housing, education
and healthcare for all. Every child in the UK has access to education and healthcare, but is the supply of food and housing
sufficient? Overcrowding in cities must not reach Dickensian
proportions again. There are very clear guidelines about how
many children should inhabit a room and how those aged over
16 should not be expected to share at all. However, in Kensington
and Chelsea these are not being followed, resulting in serious
overcrowding.

'Child poverty in UK at highest level since 2010, official
figures show. About 30% of Britain's children are now classified
as poor, of whom two-thirds are from working families,' warned
The Guardian in March 2017.

Was anyone listening? A few generations ago many people
in the UK thought theirs a country where they could
become 'self-made': they could clamber from rags to riches
through intelligence and hard work. Higher education was free

and families were starting to move across the class divides. Now, higher education is a luxury that many cannot even contemplate for their children.

I'm part of the problem

'Life is [rubbish], then you die,' goes the old phrase. For some, that statement really sums it up. However, that is reckoning without the glorious future of heaven. Heaven is a place where God's values are fully in place. We will all be equal, and sex, race, colour, education, faith and politics will no longer divide us. Remember my favourite piece of Grenfell graffiti, which boldly stated 'We are one' and conjured up so many images for me. It is reminiscent of the line from 1 Corinthians that appears in the Anglican communion service: 'We are one body, because we all share in one bread' (*CW*, p. 179). Christians, in essence, believe we are all equal because Jesus died for everyone in the world. The graffiti artist was right. We are all human, we are all suffering, we are one community. The truth remains that we are all one humanity, rich or poor.

Yet we long to be different from others, better than others. We use external factors like skin colour or we create artificial reasons to make ourselves feel superior to those who are on the same rung on the metaphorical ladder of life: my children got into the grammar school; he belongs to a different tribe from mine; we holiday in Bournemouth, not Blackpool. We constantly try to drag ourselves up, and consequently push others down.

I wonder what the world would look like if we all treated our fellow humans the same, no matter who they were. I once went into a café and was trying to suss out their cakes, but received no assistance from the serving staff because they were taking selfies with a slim, bearded man. I was very frustrated and started to leave, when I suddenly realized who he was: Russell Brand, bad boy and film actor. If we were all equal, I would have eaten my cake there that day. As it was, I went elsewhere.

The challenge I face is to treat everyone well all the time, no matter who they are.

I have an amazing Aussie friend called Claire who has taught me so much about welcoming people. She has a beaming smile and walks up to strangers with a 'Hi, I'm Claire!' It's not hard to do, but yet, as a grumpy Brit, it's not natural to me to be so polite, kind, friendly, confident. The effect of how she treats people is that they feel good – and I want to make that happen too. If you believe we are all equal in God's eyes, you can live it out by treating everyone the same.

I realize that I am part of the greater problem, however. As someone who is privileged to have had a university education, who has never struggled to put food on the table and who relates to many of those in power, I know I could have done more prior to the fire. I knew people in the Tower, but I had never assisted them in any way or advocated for them. I knew there were fire safety concerns about Grenfell and what did I do? Nothing. I listened, and I said, 'That sounds terrible – they should do something about that.' My question to myself is: who are 'they' and what did I think they should have done? I could have been part of them in doing something. But I wasn't.

I was me, sinful, selfish, well intentioned, overbusy. For that I can repent and receive forgiveness. I see that I have a share of the blame; I am a part of the system that allowed this to happen.

As human beings, we are all part of this mess in the world and sometimes we are victims of other people's mess! We can all look back on times when we did something and it was only by God's grace there wasn't a terrible outcome: perhaps the time we drove carelessly on the motorway and could have caused a massive pile-up killing dozens of people; or that time we let our child's hand slip because we were checking our phone and he raced into the road, which was mercifully clear of cars. When I come face to face with my sin and shortcomings, I can start to become part of the solution.

As a Christian I am trying to do what I feel called to do and direct my efforts into projects on which I can see God's hand. This book is one example. I have access to local resources without having to make contacts. I was already embedded into this community, and that has given me access to places I wouldn't have been able to go unless I was resident here and shared to some degree in the suffering.

My theology shows me that humans are fallen: we have made wrong choices from the beginning of time and we continue to make bad decisions. We can be selfish and lazy, and we often try to do the right thing for the wrong reasons. However, Jesus is the perfect human being. He is God in human form and he showed us how to live. He was provocative in how he lived, challenging people in his responses to seemingly innocent questions, and breaking accepted religious protocol. He was love personified.

He willingly gave himself up and refused to defend himself when falsely accused, even though he knew that would seal his death sentence. He died for the world, and through his example we see others also prepared to die for what they believe in, not through suicide bombs or destruction but by tackling evil face to face, with love, courage and generosity.

The gospel (the word simply means 'good news') is that Jesus gave us access to a holy God although we are lowly, selfish and sinful. We all know that we do wrong. 'If we say we have no sin, we deceive ourselves, and the truth is not in us' (1 John 1.8 ESV). *But* even a sinful person is made right with God through the sacrifice of Jesus! This is why it is such good news. All those who have cheated or lied, even those who have concealed their own part in the Grenfell disaster, have access to grace and a hope for the future. God has used people in prisons before now to do his work!

Your hope and future

What about you? What is your calling? What assets do you have? What issues do you care about? You don't have to save the world single-handedly (Jesus has already done that) but you can make a difference to your world. What really angers you? What do you want to change?

'After Grenfell I found my voice,' I heard one resident say. He was then able to speak up for what he believed when previously he would have remained silent.

In Chapter 10 Esmé Page had an insistent voice in her head telling her what to do. She personifies 2 Corinthians 3.12: 'since we have such a hope, we are very bold.' It wasn't easy to do what she did, but when she stepped out, God stepped in.

Zoe LeVack from Kids on the Green saw things that horrified her and it pushed her to act, and the project became something far bigger than she had imagined.

Montrise Eastmond-Lewis saw a problem and had skills and contacts that she could use to help people. Playing the steel pans is a very specific gift! But perhaps that is not your area of expertise. You might be able to knit squares for baby blankets in hospitals, or bungee jump to raise awareness of suffering seabirds. Whatever it is that you enjoy can be coupled with something you are passionate about to make a difference. You can bring hope too.

In our area, the churches, community centres and mosque simply opened their doors and welcomed people in. You too can welcome people, not necessarily into your home, but in the way you greet them and treat them.

Perhaps you are exhausted and the idea of doing anything is too much. My message to you is to hang on. There is hope and there is love. Jesus loves you and he believes in you; he has plans to give you hope and a future. I pray you will meet hope bearers who point you in the direction of those who can help you. It's not possible for us all to feel great all the time, but the Christian life is one that can hold out light and hope to those who are suffering. The apostle Paul tells us, 'Now hope that is seen is not hope. For who hopes for what he sees?' (Romans 8.24 ESV). The very point of hope is that it hasn't happened yet, but holding it in front of you helps it to guide you and perhaps become a reality. Kids on the Green achieved its goal. After it was set up, I did not see any children wandering aimlessly around, looking at memory walls. What I did see was a group of very busy, happy children, playing together and having fun in difficult times.

Not all the hope bearers interviewed above were Christians, because hope is not exclusively Christian. There are millions of people from all faiths and none who bear hope. These people can be found everywhere: children selling badges to raise money for a cause they believe in, men working with brain trauma patients, women starting businesses so that children in their village can be educated . . . so please do not misunderstand me. However, hope is intrinsically Christian. Christians have a gospel of hope to share and, as a Christian, I am keen to promote this!

I used to work in an office with a thriving sales team. They had posters adorning their walls with motivational phrases. One such was 'Persistence wears down resistance'. The persistence that I recommend is one where you keep your goal ahead of you and refuse to give up. If your goal is God-given, it will endure. If your courage and perseverance are wearing thin, you need to surround yourself with people who believe the same thing as you and are working together for the same goal. Encouragement and shared vision motivate us to continue.

The Bible exhorts us to stand up for those whose voice is not loud enough to be heard:

> Speak up for those who cannot speak for themselves,
>   for the rights of all who are destitute.
> Speak up and judge fairly;
>   defend the rights of the poor and needy.
>
> (Proverbs 31.8–9)

This passage from the book of Proverbs is clear in its demands. It involves speaking up *and* judging fairly. If someone is poor, that doesn't automatically mean that he or she is right, but it certainly doesn't mean that he or she is wrong. It is often those who are in more extreme circumstances who have thought carefully about their situation and what led to it. When I interviewed Jimmy Bracher he didn't need to sit for hours mulling over the answers to my questions; he has lived in social housing all his life, and he knows the peaks and the troughs. He has reflected on his future and what is best for his family, and that is why he was able to answer so thoughtfully.

Each of us is powerful. We are not hopeless and we are not useless. Our voice is important, and in these days of social media we can make or break a company based on our feedback alone. If you found a rat in your hotel bed and took a photo of it, that hotel might well cease to operate! If a politician is accused of sexual misconduct, he or she may feel obliged to resign – or may not! Those who have been ground down, abused and mistreated often feel powerless. That is when members of the community need to step in with their united voices, especially those who are privileged, to speak for those who can't speak for themselves or for those whose voices are ignored or not believed because of their situations. When we take on the institutions we have a fight on our hands and often one we are not equipped to win alone!

Ten weeks after Grenfell, people started to talk about healing. Most of the solutions were therapeutic – hand massages, reiki and so on – but actual healing will only occur through forgiveness. A massage will relieve stress for a while but it will return. The Christian message is to forgive the guilty, or those you perceive to be guilty, even when they don't repent. Forgiveness is as much a gift from us to ourselves as it is to them. When we release the blame, we feel better: the bitterness goes and we receive peace. This does not mean letting people off the hook for gross misconduct, but it does mean releasing them to God and not hating them. It is a question of seeking justice without malice.

North Kensington is just one area in one borough in one city. Our story has been broadcast worldwide, exposing the atrocious housing situation and conditions operating here. The council officials were shamed and the world saw that. The Government had to step in and take the power away from them. They have been humbled and now they have to move forward. The challenge is set, but will they rise to it? Only time will tell.

Challenges to the individual

Why is it that we can walk past a homeless person on the street and not even look at him or her, but when we see a burning building we want to help out and buy brand-new things for these people who had but have no longer? What blinds us to one person's suffering and allows us to wallow in another's? Do we judge people? Do we think, *It's clearly that homeless man's fault he is homeless, so it's acceptable to ignore him*? Or perhaps we see him doing the same thing every day and as we see no progression we judge that he isn't worth our pity, or we are ashamed and embarrassed that we have no words to say. Perhaps by pretending he isn't there or that it's his fault, we can soothe our guilty consciences.

We are not without resources. If you see a homeless person, you can say 'hello' and you can welcome that man or woman into your life by sharing your name. You can share your lunch with him or her; you don't have to make a grand gesture. Ignoring a fellow human being is the worst thing you can do because you are treating a person like an inanimate object.

Another curiosity is the great generosity we have in the UK for large-scale charity drives such as Children in Need or Comic Relief. It is often those who could themselves benefit from the money who raise the most for others or even give generously. What motivates us to give some things to some people and not to others? God has created us with love in our hearts and compassion. When the compassion is awoken by images of suffering people or by actually meeting them, it motivates us to try and help, but it is sometimes our own prejudices that define the type of person we feel is deserving of help.

Aid agencies often send their employees to the countries where they operate, in order to motivate them in their jobs when they see the real needs of genuine people. If we can see that what we are doing makes a difference to actual people, rather than a faceless mass, we are more likely to work with focus and passion. God has created us to see and feel. He wants us to reach out with our arms and hold people. He wants the sight of things to have an impact on us, and he wants us to bring justice to his world by living generously and openly. Giving is good for us. We read in 2 Corinthians 9.6: 'Remember this: whoever sows sparingly will also reap sparingly, and whoever sows generously will also reap generously.' Those who give to a good cause will get a return, although not necessarily financially. This verse shows us that as we give, according to what we have decided in our heart we will get a return.

When we give, we release good to someone other than ourselves, and that feels amazing. However, if we try to give and it is thrown back in our faces, that can be a terrible blow because it takes our joy. Perhaps part of the reason why people sometimes reject help is a 'power thing'. They may think, *If I give to you, the power is in my hands; but if I am always the taker, I submit to you.* However, that is not the case. Pride too can often stop people from receiving the generosity others offer to them, because they want to be self-reliant. In a community that functions well, we should be able to share what we have without causing offence if it is done gently and quietly. If you are prepared to receive, you give the gift of joy to the person who is giving.

Raise your eyes. I urge you to raise your expectations of God, of his care for you and all he has for you. Connect with the one who powers the universe and you will see great things. Connect with a calling or a plan from on high, where heaven meets earth, and be awestruck by what can be achieved. Work with others on a shared dream to change the world, and you never know where your tiny idea may take you.

We in North Kensington are already on this journey. The destination is unknown, but I have hope in my heart that somehow this tragedy will be a catalyst in the UK for justice for the poor. May those who are privileged speak up for those who are powerless. May the love which has been poured out in the aftermath of Grenfell extend further still, reaching beyond momentary compassion to become a lasting love that touches other dispossessed and broken souls. If you want to join me, sign here on the dotted line: ....

Every voice counts, and every person is important, as we set about the many small changes that will make life better for others. It's not easy, but it is a divine calling. We don't travel alone.

Conclusion

Sometimes the horror of what I've seen and experienced hits me like a ton of bricks. I want my old life back, the life where the most important thing in my life was getting the kids to school in a clean uniform and feeding them three times a day. The life where I didn't have to contemplate my neighbours lying dead in a pile of ashes. These are the times it really hurts and I think I'm cracking up. I used to have conversations in my head, and wondered if I was going mad, but that's not true. It's perfectly normal for grief to feel like this. Last week I was angry; this week I am sad. Sometimes I feel a bit of both and I want to take it out on someone. At times I have wanted to rant and scream and make up conspiracy theories so there is someone to blame, someone to hate, someone who will pay for all this death and destruction.

I hate conspiracy theories, but do I blame people for having them? No, I don't. These are days when others' pain and suffering counts. My pain and suffering counts, and no one outside can quite understand how it feels to be here. Moving past the horror of the building, we're beyond anger at the Council – we want justice. Some of us want revenge. I want peace for all, but peace seems a long way off. Peace does not look like this broken, hurting community.

The most common thing I have heard people say is that they want this tragedy never to happen again. We want the authorities, the councils, the Government to learn the lesson and to be safety-conscious, to protect the lives of those they are responsible for housing, even if they spend a fortune doing it.

I want people to sit up and notice the appalling inequality in the UK. I want rich landowners, property developers and builders to create beautiful, safe housing for everyone, rich or poor. I don't want a situation where money determines how safely you sleep in your bed. I want the poor to be a matter for public concern, and not just stepped over by those who have ways of making problems disappear. I want Christians in the UK to be at the forefront of these changes. I want social justice and I don't want to stop at this country; I want to see the world a fairer place. It isn't enough to buy fair-trade products to help the world's poor, or fling a bit of money to a charity every time there is a disaster. I want God's justice to come to earth. I want to see the poor have justice, the hungry fed, and all people to have access to good food, housing, education and healthcare. I want to live in a civilized society and I have no idea how to achieve that.

This is my cost. This is my burden. This is the road of suffering that paves the way to the cross of Jesus. But beyond the cross, beyond the pain, beyond the suffering is heaven, beautiful, glorious heaven, where we will be one with God and where finally all of this craziness will make sense.

In concluding this book, I would love to tell you that those who failed to do their duties were punished, that the criminals were caught and that the world was a safe place again. But it's not that easy.

This terrible tragedy in Kensington in 2017 highlights two issues.

The first is that bad things happen and sometimes there are people making these things happen.

The second thing is that where there is tragedy, there will be people trying to make things better and heal the hurts. Hope is a real concept given to us by God to take us through pain and into a gradual healing. He uses a wide variety of people to help out and they may not be the people you expect them to be. They may be the homeless man giving his only coat, or the child who tips out her piggy bank, or the Muslim who welcomes the Christian to pray in his peaceful space, but this is real life. This is community where we share humanity despite our diversity. When the worst happened, we all grieved. Then we worked together to try and rebuild our lives and to bring comfort to those most affected.

If this translates into lasting change, there will truly be hope rising from Grenfell.

'May the God of hope fill you with all joy and peace in believing, so that by the power of the Holy Spirit you may abound in hope' (Romans 15.13 ESV).

Study guide

This book is ideal for reading with others and each chapter can be read separately.

Group questions on the book

These questions are for those who discuss the book as a whole, in one sitting:

- What place does politics have in this book? Do you agree or disagree with Gaby's political stance? Why?
- Why do you think people were so generous with their time and money during this crisis? Have you ever seen similar generosity or even participated in it?
- Have you ever felt called or led to do something tough? Did you manage to do it? If so, what motivated you to do it and to complete the task?
- Do you think we can change the world?

Group questions on individual chapters

The following questions are written for use in a small group setting, perhaps a Christian homegroup or equivalent, where you are going through each chapter individually. You can pick and choose which questions you answer and there are Bible passages suggested to help your thinking.

1 Introduction

Read this verse as an opening time of worship or prayer: Isaiah 33.2.

You can either play some quiet music in the background or sit in silence as people contemplate this verse. It grows on you!

- Do you ever remember feeling excited after an election?
- What did you hope would happen subsequently?
- Were your hopes fulfilled? Why or why not?

Read Isaiah 33.

- Here the Lord God is portrayed as an everlasting consuming fire. It is uncomfortable to read this in the light of Grenfell, but verse 18 seems even more applicable than before. Why do you think the Bible can speak so relevantly into situations that happen so long after it was written?

- This Bible chapter speaks of the promised land, and verse 22 states who is in charge! Do you ever struggle between the laws of the land and the law of God?
- Are you comforted by the promises of Isaiah 33.22–24? If not, why not?
- In the crisis Gaby says that she prayed. How do you respond in a crisis?
- Gaby speaks of the community as being 'united in grief'. Have you ever been united in grief with others or is your experience of grief more solo?
- Can you gain any encouragement from either this chapter or Isaiah 33?

Pray Isaiah 33.6 for each other.

2 Waking up

- 'Give to the one who asks you, and do not turn away from the one who wants to borrow from you' (Matthew 5.42). Jesus tells us to give as people ask of us. Do you think he meant that literally? How do you think he would want you to give, and to whom?
- In Luke 3.11 John the Baptist answers the crowd's questions by saying, 'Anyone who has two shirts should share with the one who has none, and anyone who has food should do the same.' John is encouraging a revolutionary way of sharing. Is it realistic? If not, why not?
- What do you think explains people's overwhelming generosity towards North Kensington?

When I (Gaby) was a child I was devastated by the Zeebrugge ferry disaster in 1987, in which 193 people died. I was nearly 11 years old and for the next few years I would pray for the victims' families every night. I feel that gave me a soft heart to share in the suffering of others, even those I had never met or would never meet.

- Have you ever experienced a need to help in a desperate situation? Was it a one-off or did it lead to a pattern of behaviour?
- Why do you think the Bible encourages us so frequently to give to those in need?
- In Chapter 8, 'Hope unleashed', when Fatima speaks about taking her treasure with her out of the Tower, she refers to her children. What is your treasure? 'For where your treasure is, there your heart will be also' (Matthew 6.21).

Pray that you will have your focus on the right treasure.

Alternative questions

- Gaby said, 'It was as if someone had hit "pause" on my life.' Have you ever experienced this?
- How did you cope? What helped you? What didn't help?
- How could you use this experience to help others in a similar situation?

3 The cavalry wore dog collars

Gaby's husband is a vicar and not someone who regularly does dangerous things, and she was a little nervous for his safety when he went out.

- Does someone dear to you have a job that risks his or her life on a regular basis?
- How does that feel? Do you pray about this? Does it wreck your life that your loved one has this call?
- What kind of support do you offer your loved one? What kind of support do you receive for this? Can this group offer you support?
- Have you ever considered a call to a job but been too scared to follow it up, whether that be in the emergency services or the armed forces, or even in church leadership?
- Is now the time to rethink this call?

Sean said (pages 35–6):

At the same time, there has been so much to thank God for and such a strong sense of God's presence *in* the pain. Knowing God is there doesn't necessarily diminish the loss or anger, nor should it. But it enables you to see beyond the sadness and anger, to see that even though they are so serious and overwhelming, they are not the whole story. In particular, the thing that will stay with me and which gives me hope every day is the way in which the community and people from further afield united so rapidly, and with simple compassion, to respond to the need they saw, and the way in which this meant so much to those who had been affected.

Do you agree with him? Why, or why not?

Read Romans 8.28: 'And we know that in all things God works for the good of those who love him, who have been called according to his purpose.'

- What good are you seeking?
- Are you following God's calling on your life or have you lost the path?

Pray for your calling, that it will be made clear. Pray also for those in your community who have tough callings, especially those who risk their lives daily for the good of others, that they will know God's love and peace with them.

4 Urban hope

- Have you ever shared with the group your story of how you ended up living where you live?
- Is there anything you would like to share with group members about who you are that they perhaps don't know?
- 'And who knows but that you have come to your royal position for such a time as this?' (Esther 4.14b). What is the purpose for you of being in this group?
- What do you feel others bring to the group?
- Gaby speaks about being scared of people of other faiths. Do you have any fears that hold you back from doing something God may be nudging you towards?

- Gaby speaks of Christians as holding royal position. Do you feel as a Christian that you are royalty, well considered and loved by God? Or perhaps you feel more like a cleaner in the house of God, unnoticed, unthanked and unworthy. What is the truth?

Pray for each other in the light of these revelations.

5 Hands off, it's ours!

- Which are the key local authorities in your area?
- Do people trust the authorities? Why?
- Who do you think is at the heart of your local community?
- How can the Church become more a part of that core if it is not already?

Read Psalm 127 together.

> Unless the LORD builds the house,
>   the builders labour in vain.
> Unless the LORD watches over the city,
>   the guards stand watch in vain.
>
> (Psalm 127.1)

- What part of the community is being built in vain, do you think?
- What do you think the Lord is in fact building?
- How can you be part of what the Lord is building in some small way?

Pray for yourself, your group and your church to become part of what the Lord is doing in your area.

Alternative questions

- How would you define poverty in the UK?
- What do you feel could be done to tackle poverty?
- What part of this effort could you get involved in?

6 Short stories of hope

- Which of the short stories of hope touched you most? Why?
- What do you think is the purpose of cataloguing such small stories?
- Did you feel encouraged to read these stories or did you feel that they were of little consequence?
- Have you ever done a small thing that has had a large positive consequence?

Read Colossians 3.22–25:

> Slaves, obey your earthly masters in everything; and do it, not only when their eye is on you and to curry their favour, but with sincerity of heart and reverence for the Lord. Whatever you do, work at it with all your heart, as working for the Lord, not for human masters, since you know that you will receive an inheritance from the Lord as a reward. It is the Lord Christ you are serving. Anyone who does wrong will be repaid for their wrongs, and there is no favouritism.

- What do you think this passage means?
- How does it inspire you?

Pray in the light of these revelations.

7 Where the streets have no name

- Gaby speaks about the gentrification of Notting Hill. Have you ever experienced a similar thing?
- How do you think it would feel to be gradually elbowed out of the place you grew up in, and to see all your friends and family dispersed?
- Is this just the way life is or do you think this is a bigger problem?
- What do you think is the solution to this problem?

Read Psalm 133.

- Do the words in verse 1 provide a good motto for a borough to have?
- How can we live out this psalm in real life?
- What are the challenges of it?

Pray for the outworking of this psalm across your area, your country and the world.

8 Hope unleashed

- Whom do you admire in your community? Why?
- The three stories in this chapter were all very different. We were introduced to the firefighter; Fatima, the woman who escaped; and Mr Abdurahman, the chief executive of the Al Manaar Mosque. What excited or challenged you about these stories?
- Fatima's positivity and reliance on the Lord is unusual among people who have suffered so much. What challenges you about the way you live, looking at her example?

- Would you be able to assist someone of another faith in his or her worship, as Mr Abdurahman did, or would you feel uncomfortable?

Read Matthew 22.34–40.
Jesus exhorts us to love God and love others. How can we overflow with love for others who are of different faiths from our own without compromising what we believe? Jesus is the God of Christianity, and he must have a way forward for us in this age of many faiths and none.

Pray for courage, for love and for wisdom about how to love God and others in these days we live in.

9 Hope bearers

- Have you ever raged against suffering?
- If you feel able to share your experience of this raging, in what context did it happen?
- Do you believe that 'hope keeps us going'?

Read Hebrews 10.19–25.

- What do you believe the purpose of hope is?
- Do you know anyone whom you would describe as a 'hope bearer'? Who and why?
- How can you or I be a hope bearer to those around us?
- What are the desperate local needs where you live?
- Can you practise the dogged perseverance and self-giving that are required to give generously to people who are struggling?

Pray for the ability to be hope bearers to those around us. Use Hebrews 10.21–25 as a prayer for your group.

10 The world was watching

- Do you remember what you were doing when you heard about Grenfell Tower burning? What instant impact did it have on you?
- Why do you think a burning building had such an impact on so many people?
- Would the Grenfell fire have affected you so much if it had happened somewhere else in the world?
- What do you think the benefits of Cornwall Hugs Grenfell were to those who had holidays through that charity?

Read Hebrews 4.1–11.

Discuss this passage. Rest is a very key part of an active healthy life, but one we often forget.

- When have you most benefited from a holiday or a break?
- Have you ever had a retreat or a time away to rest with God?
- What were the benefits of that type of rest?

Challenge: try to take an hour of rest this week, a day of rest this month and an overnight retreat at some point in the next year.

Pray for each of you to have good rest in your lives, for you to see the point of rest and to be able to enjoy it.

11 From me to you

- What do you believe justice is?
- Gaby says, 'Rich people have choices; poor people have limits' (page 180). Do you agree with this? Have you seen this play out in life?

- What do you believe true justice would look like for Grenfell?
- What do you believe justice would look like for all the poor and oppressed in the UK?
- How are we going to get justice?
- When have you been unjust?

Read Micah 6.1–8.

- What is the challenge set to us all in this passage?
- Is it a challenge we can fulfil?

Pray that you can act justly, love mercy and walk humbly in your life.

Final questions

- What impact has reading this book had on your life (if any)?
- Have you made any resolutions or accepted any of the challenges? If so, tell someone else so that you can be accountable to one another in these things.